Forever Young

For Maya +
Dietric

Great friends
+ animal
defenders -

- Bill

Forever Young

....

*How Six Great Individuals
Have Drawn upon the Powers of
Childhood and How We Can
Follow Their Lead*

WILLIAM CRAIN

TURNING
STONE
PRESS

Cover design by Frame25 Productions
Cover art by Oksana Shufrych c/o Shutterstock.com
Print book interior design by Howie Severson

Permission to reprint excerpts from *Reason for Hope*
by Jane Goodall, Copyright © 2003, was granted
by Grand Central Publishing, an imprint of
Hachette Book Group, Inc.

Turning Stone Press
San Antonio, TX

Library of Congress Control Number
is available upon request.

ISBN 978-1-61852-136-1

10 9 8 7 6 5 4 3 2 1

To Jane Goodall

People like you and me...do not grow old no matter how long we live. What I mean is we never cease to stand like curious children before the great Mystery into which we are born.

—Albert Einstein,
Letter to Dr. Otto Juliusburger

Contents

APPENDIXES

Preface

I have long felt that people can live richer and more creative lives by recapturing the special powers of childhood. I have written this book to open readers to this possibility.

I first became aware of childhood's special qualities in the late 1960s, when my wife Ellen and I started a family. As I helped care for our growing children and got to know other children in our neighborhood, I was struck by their bold curiosity, elaborate make-believe play, and love of nature. I began to think about how these qualities get lost in the process of growing up and how adults might benefit by reclaiming them.

As I was considering these matters, I was also beginning an academic career in developmental psychology. To my disappointment, my profession had little to say about the special qualities of the young. Instead, developmental psychologists focused on children's acquisition of adult skills and knowledge. My colleagues assumed that adult competence was the preeminent goal, and the task of research was to determine how the child makes progress toward this goal. Psychologists didn't wonder if childhood might possess unique attributes that are worth retaining.

By emphasizing the child's progress toward adulthood, psychologists have reflected the values of our wider society. We have traditionally praised children for mature behavior. We have been especially enthusiastic about those who seem headed for successful careers. Indeed, our focus on the child's adult future has been so strong that when we first meet a child, one of our favorite questions is, "What do you want to be when you grow up?"

I will say more about the attitudes of psychology and the wider society in the introduction. Here I want to note that over the years I did find psychologists and other scholars who valued the adult application of the qualities of childhood. These writers were scarce, but their work encouraged me to keep looking into the topic.

One of these inspirations was the pioneering developmental psychologist Heinz Werner. Werner suggested that the most creative thinkers do not begin problem-solving with adult, intellectual thought. Instead, they initially approach the world in a more naive and childlike manner. They start by paying attention to the sensations and feelings that situations or people arouse in them.

To explore Werner's idea, Ellen, a pediatrician, and I studied how her colleagues evaluated infants brought to an emergency room with a fever. The doctors wanted to determine whether the infants were seriously ill. We found that the most esteemed diagnosticians, in contrast to the others, did try to obtain a feeling-sense of the babies' health before proceeding to more rational analyses.

I also have found inspiration in the work of two contemporary psychologists. Howard Gardner has called attention to the beauty and vitality of young children's artistic activities, and he has described how modern artists have tried to recapture the outlook of children.

The second psychologist is Louise Chawla. Chawla has conducted research on my own strongest interest—children's feelings for nature—and has shown how adults can revive these feelings for their own emotional well-being.

In this book, I describe how the distinctive capacities of childhood have contributed to the life and work of six great individuals: The naturalists Henry David Thoreau and Rachel Carson, the physicist Albert Einstein, the novelist Charlotte Brontë, the minister Howard Thurman, and the primate researcher Jane Goodall. In various ways, these scholars have drawn on their childhood enthusiasm for play, sense of wonder, and oneness with nature.

To an extent, these individuals represent a variety of professions. But I also selected people who have made a strong personal impression on me. As a result, the group is slanted toward individuals who have maintained or renewed their childhood love of nature.

I believe that my emphasis on feelings for nature is more than a personal bias. From their earliest years, children gain inspiration from nature. Many of their drawings and poems are about animals and nature, and their make-believe play is richest when it takes place in natural settings. When children spend time in nature, they gain feelings of calm and belonging to the larger web of life. It makes sense, then, that adults might wish to recapture their childhood ties to the natural world.

In any event, I look forward to the study of a wider range of adults who have drawn on the remarkable powers of childhood. The knowledge gained might inspire more readers to reach back to their childhoods to enrich their lives.

Introduction

· · · · · · ·

Invisible Children

> *I am invisible, understand, simply because people refuse to see me.*
>
> —Ralph Ellison

This book takes up a novel proposal: that adults can productively call upon the strengths of childhood. Few have written on the topic. The main reason for this omission is that people have been slow to recognize that children do, in fact, possess unique strengths. Indeed, Western society has frequently overlooked the nature of childhood altogether. Let's first look at this blindness to childhood in general and then discuss children's special strengths.

Ignoring Childhood

The failure to recognize the nature of children dates back at least to the Middle Ages. In his book *Centuries of Childhood*, the French historian Philippe Ariès described how medieval society simply viewed children as miniature adults. Painters, for example, routinely depicted children with adult body proportions and facial characteristics. The children were distinguished only by their smaller size.

In medieval social life, too, children were treated like adults. By the age of six or seven, they were frequently sent off to other villages to begin working as apprentices. They learned carpentry, farming, domestic service, and other trades on the job. In their leisure hours, the children played the same games as the adults and even joined the grown-ups in the taverns.

Ariès acknowledged that adults recognized the need for protection and care of those under the age of six or seven. But overall, people seem to have paid little attention to the nature of children. No one bothered to study, for example, young children's developing speech or physical benchmarks.

As we look back on this "little adult" view of the past, it's easy to consider it quaint and antiquated. But we often lapse into it, as for example when we expect young children to sit as still as we do, or when we assume that they have the adult capacity to resist grabbing attractive objects in the grocery store. There seems to be a natural adult egocentrism, a tendency to perceive children as just like us.

In any event, the paradigm of children as little adults gradually lost its dominance. The key factor, beginning in the sixteenth century, was the changing occupational world. With the introduction of the printing press, the growth of commerce, and the rise of cities, the workplace began to take on more of a "white collar" look. New opportunities arose for lawyers, bankers, and government officials—occupations the required reading, writing, and math. A rising middle class didn't want their children to enter adult society at age six or seven. They wanted their children to get an education first. They wanted to prepare them for a brighter future. To meet this demand, schools sprouted up everywhere, and the upshot was a new view of childhood. Children were seen less as *little adults* and more as *future adults*.

Thus began the modern view of childhood. Today, few people would argue with the importance of preparing children for the future. But the modern attitude hasn't radically expanded the awareness of childhood—of a time of life when interests, outlooks, and capacities are different from those of adults. More often, the focus on a child's future has blinded people to the nature of childhood. This focus is epitomized by the standards movement, which dominates contemporary education.

The Standards Movement

The standards movement in the United States began in the late 1970s as a response to the country's economic worries. Japan, West Germany, and other countries were challenging U.S. economic superiority, and political and corporate leaders blamed the educational system. The schools, U.S. leaders said, were failing to prepare children for the new high-tech workplace. The leaders called for higher academic standards and increased standardized testing to measure students' progress.

This rhetoric sounded good, but as the standards movement gained momentum, the increase in standardized testing diminished children's enthusiasm for learning. In order to prepare students for the tests, teachers had to limit time for the activities that children found exciting and meaningful, like mock trials, writing newsletters, and the arts. Instead, children had to work on dreary test prep drills and exercises. And as testing dates approached, many children became very anxious. Testing was turning school into a miserable place.

I decided to try to do something about it. In 1988, I got elected to my local school board in Teaneck, New Jersey, and discussed testing with people in my school district. I also took the issue to the state school boards association, talked to state officials, and testified at numerous state-organized public hearings.

As I made my points, some people—especially teachers—agreed with me. But my advocacy didn't have much impact. State education officials were particularly unresponsive, and I was surprised by their reaction. These officials didn't simply disagree; rather, they looked at me with blank or quizzical expressions. They didn't seem to know what I was even talking about.

I couldn't make sense of their response for several years. Then, in 1995, I read an essay by education professor Jeffrey Kane. Kane pointed out that whereas the standards movement's documents were deeply concerned about preparing children for the future economy, the documents ignored children themselves—their needs, capacities, and interests. He called the standards movement, "Education in the Absence of Children."

Kane's essay, then, suggested a reason why my ideas produced so many puzzled expressions. I was talking a great deal about children, especially their feelings about learning. But in the world of the state education officials promoting the standards movement, children didn't factor in. They were largely invisible. I might as well have been talking about imaginary beings.

I served on the school board until 1997. Since then, this blindness to childhood has persisted. In fact, it has become more prevalent for the youngest students.

Two studies—one by Diane Levin and Judith Van Hoorn, the other by Clarke Fowler—reveal that today's kindergartens and many preschools are heavily academic and pay little attention to the spontaneous interests of their charges. Children have few opportunities for activities they love—play, the arts, and the exploration of nature. Instead, they are forced to cope with formal academics and tests they can barely fathom. Many youngsters become anxious or angry. Others turn off and become listless.

Many veteran kindergarten and preschool teachers are upset by the premature academics, but they report that no one is listening to them. Schools are devoted to high test scores, and most administrators insist that teachers stick to step-by-step curricula designed to produce good scores. In this environment, children's own interests and passions don't enter the picture.

Parents

Within the standards movement, then, an indifference to children can be extreme. Is this indifference also common among parents?

There isn't systemic research on this question, but it's my impression that many parents, like the veteran teachers I mentioned, do pay attention to children. They see how the tests upset their children and turn their children off to school. Parents miss the exuberance with which children played, sang, and drew before they were forced to deal with test-driven schooling.

These parental concerns have contributed to a revolt called the "opt out" movement. In 2015, significant minorities of parents in New York, Colorado, and a few other states encouraged their third- to eighth-grade children to not take the tests aligned with the new Common Core standards. In New York, about 20 percent of the students opted out, a number that remained fairly constant over the next three years.

So parents, compared to standards advocates, may be paying more attention to children. But parents' attention is divided. Although they are concerned about their children's feelings and interests in the present moment, they also worry about their children's futures. They want their children to get into the best colleges and have successful careers. Hoping to give their children a competitive start, they try to teach their children concepts and provide lots of information, beginning in infancy. And they want their children to keep moving forward, developing new intellectual and social skills. They dread the prospect that their youngsters will fall behind. The result is that parents are so busy teaching their children new things that they don't give full attention to children's own, spontaneous interests. And they fail to see how children, pursuing these interests, demonstrate remarkable powers—including the capacity for wonder.

Ignoring Wonder

The sense of wonder has impressed sages throughout the ages. Plato said wonder was the source of all philosophy. Goethe called wonder "the highest to which man can attain."

In experiences of wonder we marvel at what we perceive. We also feel a sense of mystery—a sense that there is always more to discover.

In 1954, the psychologist Abraham Maslow identified wonder as one of the distinguishing characteristics of highly creative individuals. His biographical studies suggested that such individuals perceive everyday sights—a flower, a sunset, an infant—as amazing and fascinating. Creative people don't like to judge and classify from the outset; instead, they behold every object as special and unique. And they love to view them from different angles, appreciating their infinite richness.

Such perception, Maslow added, is rare in adults but common in children. Children experience the world "intently, absorbed, spellbound, popeyed, enchanted."

But adults frequently overlook the child's sense of wonder. Or, when they do see it, they don't fully appreciate it.

Let me give some examples.

I saw a girl, about two years old, stop on a walk with her mother to look at two puppies who were vigorously playing. The child stood perfectly still, watching in amazement. After a minute or so, the child quietly said, "Two dogs," and she kept staring, totally enthralled. The mother, however, saw an opportunity to present an educational song—a "twos song." She coaxed the girl into singing "Two dogs, two cows, two horses," and so on. The child reluctantly joined in, and the mother pulled her away.

Perhaps the mother strengthened the little girl's concept of two and her vocabulary, but she cut short the child's silent wonder. I doubt the mother recognized how enraptured the child was.

Similar adult behavior is routine at the farm sanctuary that my wife Ellen and I founded. Young children typically look at the animals in amazement. But instead of just standing back and appreciating the children's enchantment, the caregivers try to direct and teach the children. The adults say: "Say Hi to the chicken, Jill." "Johnny, do you remember the sound a duck makes? Can you make the duck sound?" "Tell me, Jack, which are hens and which are roosters?" The adults distract the children from their enthralled state.

Childhood wonder can often be observed at the beach. For example, toddlers (one- and two-year-olds) are fascinated by the sand. They touch it, pat it, and run it through their fingers. They are completely absorbed. They act as if the sand holds the secret to some cosmic mystery.

I have seen toddlers explore sand for over an hour, but usually caregivers cut their explorations short. Sometimes caregivers interrupt children to clean their hands. Joan Erikson described another adult intervention, which I also have observed on many occasions: The adult walks over and instructs the child on the use of a toy shovel and bucket. The toddler is like a little Einstein trying to unravel a profound mystery, but the adult isn't impressed. The adult urges the toddler to do something more "advanced," to build something with conventional toys.

When gazing at animals or exploring sand, young children are usually quiet. They are completely engrossed. So they don't give us verbal clues regarding the source of their fascination. But if Maslow was correct, their perception is likely to be richer than ours. We typically see an object, label it, and go on to something else. Young children, in contrast, are so enchanted that they may perceive many aspects that we overlook. And the object is so wonderful to them that they want to learn more about it.

Academics' Blind Spots

I have been critical of parents for ignoring the child's sense of wonder. But scholars and researchers also have been slow to recognize it. My field of psychology dates back to the 1800s, but it wasn't until the 1950s that leading psychologists like Maslow and Ernest Schachtel wrote about the child's sense of wonder.

Other remarkable childhood strengths include:

- the boldness of the toddler's explorations

- children's empathy for animals and feelings of oneness with nature

- the richness of young children's make-believe play

- the beauty of young children's drawings

- young children's amazing ability to acquire syntax, the complex rules for creating and understanding sentences

In each case, the ordinary child's capacity exceeds that of most adults. And in each case, it has taken researchers a long time to recognize the unique strength. Like most adults, researchers have generally viewed the child as a work in progress, gradually developing the cognitive and social skills of the adult. The special strengths of childhood have largely escaped researchers' notice. (For readers who wish to know more about these strengths, I have provided a synopsis in Appendix B.)

The Importance of Seeing the Child

If adults can see children more clearly, children will benefit. As adults recognize the remarkable nature of many childhood capacities, they will give children more opportunities to develop them, and children will become more fulfilled and creative.

We also need to see children more clearly for our own sake as adults. Our lives have frequently become dull and stagnant. One way to get out of our malaise is to become more childlike. For example, we can renew a childlike wonder at the miracle of nature. If we pay attention to wonder and other special qualities in children, we will be in a better position to recapture these qualities.

This Book

In an earlier book (*Reclaiming Childhood*), I wrote about the first goal—giving children opportunities to develop the special strengths of the childhood years. The present book, my sequel, deals with the contributions of childhood qualities to adult lives.

I will first describe how childhood strengths have helped six great individuals: the naturalists Henry David Thoreau and Rachel Carson, the physicist Albert Einstein, the novelist Charlotte Brontë, the minister Howard Thurman, and the primate researcher Jane Goodall. In various ways, childhood wonder, playfulness, and sensitivity to nature have enabled them to overcome personal roadblocks and create great works.

I hope that my discussions of these creative giants will convince readers that they, too, should be alert to the powers of childhood and call upon them. In the second part of this book, I will offer suggestions about how readers might become more childlike and thereby lead more open, creative, and energetic lives.

Finally, two appendixes are designed for readers who wish to delve further into topics I have raised. The first provides a historical sketch of pioneering scholars' views on the recovery of childhood strengths. The second appendix summarizes the research to date on these strengths.

‹ *Part I* ›

Six Lives

⇌ 1 ⇌

Henry David Thoreau

. . . .

Recapturing the Fresh Senses of a Child

*I yearn for one of those old, meandering, dry, unin-
habited roads, which lead away from towns ... There
I can walk, and recover the lost child that I am.*

—Thoreau

Henry David Thoreau saw people as very unhappy.
They were earning a living, but not really living.
They had amusements, but they were suffering from an
underlying despair. As Thoreau wrote, "The mass of men
lead lives of quiet desperation."

Thoreau's personal solution was to reduce contact
with society and live in closer harmony with nature. He
spent two years in a cabin he built at Walden Pond, and
during most of his adult life he walked several hours a
day in the woods and meadows. He kept a daily journal
in which he described the ways nature invigorated him.
Many of these journal entries are so vivid that readers feel
they are outdoors with him. Thoreau's friend Bronson

Alcott said Thoreau's words seemed "scented of mountain and field breezes and rippling springs."

Thoreau didn't want others to copy his particular lifestyle; he felt individuals must find their own way. As he put it, an individual who doesn't keep pace with others might hear "a different drummer" and should "step to the music he hears, however measured or far away." At the same time, Thoreau urged people in general to get in tune with the natural world for the sake of their health and happiness.

Ultimately, Thoreau believed, nature's effect on us has a spiritual quality. Nature's ordinary inhabitants—such as birds, crickets, and flowers—convey the miracle of life. But nature only reveals her magical qualities if we adopt a certain attitude. We need to approach nature in an unhurried, loving way—and through the fresh perceptions of a child.

We'll discuss these attitudes in more detail after a review of Thoreau's life.

Thoreau's Life

Early Years

Henry David Thoreau (1817–1862) was born in Concord, Massachusetts, where he lived most of his life. He was the third of four children. Henry's father was an emotionally reserved man who worked as a shopkeeper and later ran a pencil manufacturing business. Henry's mother, a much more dynamic individual, was deeply involved in community affairs and founded the Concord Women's Anti-Slavery Society. Both parents loved nature and encouraged this love in their children.

Henry attended Miss Wheeler's "infant school"—basically a home-run day care—and then the town's public grammar school. At the age of eleven, he enrolled in the Concord Academy, a new, private college-preparatory school. He did well in his schoolwork, but he felt the place to be confining. He wrote in his journal,

> I remember how glad I was when I was kept from school a half a day to pick huckleberries on a neighboring hill . . . A half day of liberty like that was like the promise of life eternal. It was emancipation in New England. Oh, what a day was there, my countrymen!

Henry didn't play much with the other children, who regarded him as standoffish. He liked to read and even more, to explore the nearby woods, meadows, and streams. He was skilled with his hands and built his own rowboat when he was sixteen. In the summer, he liked to lie on his back in the boat in a dreamlike state, letting it take him wherever it wanted. Thoreau later wrote that this idleness made him rich, "if not in money, in sunny hours and summer days."

Encountering Grand Ideas

At his parents' urging, he attended Harvard College, even though it put a great financial strain on the family. Thoreau developed an interest in ancient literature at Harvard, but the intellectual experiences that meant the most to him were outside the college curriculum.

One such experience came during his junior year. Hoping to earn money to help pay for college, Thoreau took a leave of absence and applied for a grammar school teaching job in Canton, Massachusetts. The job interview was conducted by Orestes A. Brownson, a Unitarian minister on the school committee. During the interview Brownson, who had a high estimate of his own ideas, described his grand vision of the future. He foresaw a new day when people would be guided by an inner spiritual force that they also could perceive in nature. The interview lasted well into the night, as the two men enthusiastically exchanged ideas. Thoreau got the job, and the two continued their discussions in the weeks that followed. Thoreau was inspired.

A second important experience occurred after Thoreau returned to Harvard. During his senior year he came across a new book by Ralph Waldo Emerson titled *Nature*. Like Brownson, Emerson wrote about a spiritual presence in nature. But unlike Brownson, Emerson didn't believe people had to wait until the future to experience it; he thought it is already accessible to us. In woods and other natural settings, we sometimes forget our personal troubles because we sense that we are part of something higher—a Universal Being that circulates through nature and ourselves.

Brownson's and Emerson's ideas about a universal spirit were at the heart of a new philosophical movement known as Transcendentalism. The ideas clicked with those Thoreau had been forming in his own mind.

At Harvard, Thoreau earned sufficiently good grades to be invited to read an essay at commencement. He argued that the pursuit of wealth promotes selfishness; it is better to live a moral, independent life and value nature. Nature, Thoreau added, is much more than physical resources. It is "more beautiful than it is useful; it is more to be admired and enjoyed than used." To nourish our souls, it would be ideal if we worked only one day a week and spent the other six days drinking in nature's "soft influences and sublime revelations."

A few months after he graduated, Thoreau became friends with Emerson, who had recently moved to Concord. Emerson was fourteen years Thoreau's senior and already a famous essayist and lecturer. Seeing great promise in the young Thoreau, Emerson invited him to informal discussion groups on Transcendentalism, groups that included Brownson, Alcott, Margaret Fuller, and other forward-looking thinkers.

Thoreau was deeply impressed by Emerson; he was stirred by Emerson's ideas and accepted much of Emerson's literary advice. For a while, Thoreau even seemed to imitate Emerson's mannerisms. But the two men frequently quarreled and had an on-again, off-again relationship.

One can find several of Emerson's ideas in Thoreau's works, but their writings also took different paths. Whereas Emerson's writing was general and abstract, Thoreau focused on down-to-earth, personal experiences.

Occupations

Thoreau's first job after college was as a public school teacher, but the job didn't last long. On his tenth day, one of the school's directors visited Thoreau's class and, seeing it was noisy, called Thoreau into the corridor and ordered him to use physical punishment. Thoreau hated the practice but to comply with the command he impulsively struck two students on their open palms with a ferule (a flat stick). That evening he handed in his resignation. The next day he returned to his class and explained to his students that he couldn't teach if he had to use force—it was against his conscience.

Failing to find another teaching job, he opened his own school for a few students. Soon after, he was hired by the Concord Academy and was able to bring his older brother, John, on board as another instructor. The two taught according to their educational ideals; instead of trying to cram information into students' heads, they sought to ignite students' love of learning. They frequently took the pupils on field trips into the woods and into the town to observe jobs such as typesetting. Thoreau taught himself surveying so he could introduce it to the students, making math more relevant for them. The school flourished, but after two and half years John became extremely ill and Thoreau became too distraught to continue teaching.

Nine months later, John died of lockjaw. Thoreau became very depressed and developed sympathetic symptoms of imagined lockjaw in himself. In her recent biography, Linda Dassow Walls suggests that Thoreau came out of this emotional crisis by intensifying his exploration of nature—a passion John had shared with him.

In order to spend time in nature, Thoreau tried to limit his employment, but he actually possessed a variety of occupational skills. He became adept at surveying and took on numerous jobs. He also helped his father with his pencil manufacturing business. In fact, Thoreau greatly improved the lead in the pencils and turned the business into a competitive venture. In addition, he took on odd jobs such as carpentry and house painting, some of which he performed in exchange for room and board in the home of the Emerson family.

Walden Pond

In 1845, at the age of twenty-seven, Thoreau embarked on the experiment for which he is best known. He built a small cabin next to Walden Pond, two miles from town, to live a simple, self-sufficient existence. He wanted to discover the bare necessities of life stripped of social excesses. Growing his own vegetables—and selling some—he found he could support himself by working at temporary jobs only six weeks a year.

Thoreau still had a social life, receiving visitors and making trips to town, but he spent most of his time taking leisurely walks in nature and writing in his journal. The result of his two-year stay at Walden Pond was his book *Walden*, published in 1854. The book received several good reviews and sold moderately well in Thoreau's lifetime. It eventually sold millions of copies and became an American classic.

Visitors described Thoreau as a rugged-looking man. One said he was "straight as a pine tree," with "a strong nose that dominated his face," and "eyes as keen as an eagle's." He was a bit shorter than average, with a full beard.

Socially, he was awkward and even ornery. When news spread about his experiment at Walden Pond and his extensive knowledge of plants and animals, people wanted to visit him. He accommodated them the best he could, but this wasn't easy for him. He rarely took anyone with him on the walks he enjoyed so much.

Although Thoreau's irascibility was off-putting, he had one friend who wasn't upset by it. This was A. Bronson Alcott. Alcott—who was the father of Louisa May Alcott, author of *Little Women*—was an impractical dreamer. He established innovative schools, but they all failed. He helped create a utopian agricultural community, but he paid little attention to the finances and this venture collapsed as well. Thoreau recognized Alcott's shortcomings but valued his warm heart and intellectual tolerance. When he was with Alcott, Thoreau felt free to express new ideas even while they were still vague in his mind. The two spent many happy hours thinking up solutions to the world's problems. (For more on Alcott and his ideas, see Appendix B.)

Although he was ill at ease with most adults, Thoreau had excellent rapport with children. They listened attentively to his descriptions of wildlife and frequently brought him eggs they found in the woods. He gladly identified the species for them and then urged them to return the eggs to their nests.

A seventeen-year-old friend of the Alcott family visited Walden Pond with four younger children and later wrote that Thoreau told them all, "Keep very still and I will show you my family." Thoreau then gave a low, curious whistle and a woodchuck came running toward him from a nearby burrow. With different whistles, he summoned squirrels and birds, including a crow who nestled on his shoulder. He fed each animal with his hand and petted it gently as the youngsters gazed on in delight. He then gave a series of new low whistles and each animal departed. After this, he took the young people on a boat ride to see the lilies.

Basically, Thoreau biographer Walter Harding says, "Thoreau was a boy at heart. As he himself once commented, he never lost his sense of wonder."

Thoreau greatly admired Native Americans, observing that they "stood nearer to wild nature than we." The writer Nathaniel Hawthorne, who knew Thoreau well, said that Thoreau possessed an uncanny knack for finding the Indians' old arrowheads and relics. Hawthorne said, "it was as if their spirits willed him to be the inheritor of their simple wealth."

Thoreau recognized that he didn't fit in with modern society, and he didn't want to. He felt that the more we become immersed in society, the less we see of nature and the universe. The essence of nature is her wildness, but our social institutions—our schools, governments, and businesses—domesticate our outlooks and interests. They keep us indoors, thinking about our relations with other people—not the mysterious and beautiful natural world. That is where he spent as much time as possible.

Emerson believed that Thoreau lacked ambition and was squandering his talents. Thoreau, Emerson lamented, would be content to be "the captain of a huckleberry party." Not until after Thoreau's death did Emerson appreciate his friend's achievements.

In one journal entry, Thoreau admitted that he felt momentarily depressed by a lack of social recognition. But he said the simple rustling of an oak leaf or a bird's singing could restore his happiness. "Nature," he wrote, "is always encouraging."

Thoreau used his social detachment in the service of humor, making wry observations about society and institutions—and sometimes himself. He made these remarks to others in person and in letters and other writings. The sidebar presents a small sample of his dry humor.

~

A Sample of Thoreau's Humor

Thoreau's first book, *A Week on the Concord and Merrimack Rivers*, was a commercial failure. When the publisher returned 706 copies to him, Thoreau wrote, "I have now a library of nearly nine hundred volumes, over seven hundred of which I wrote myself."

When Emerson remarked on the need for great poets, Thoreau said he had found one in the woods, but it had feathers and had not been to Harvard.

While living at Walden Pond, he found that, "It is not necessary that a man earn his living by the sweat of his brow, unless he sweats easier than I do."

Thoreau observed that, "We are in great haste to construct a magnetic telegraph from Maine to Texas; but Maine and Texas, it may well be, have nothing important to communicate."

As he lay dying, his Aunt Louisa asked him if he had made his peace with God. He answered, "I did not know we had ever quarreled."

~

Civil Disobedience

One summer day during Thoreau's second year at Walden Pond, an unexpected event occurred. As he walked to town to pick up a mended shoe, he was met by Sam Staples, the local constable, tax collector, and jailer. Staples told him to either agree to pay his back taxes or go to jail. Thoreau chose jail.

The amounts owed were for a poll tax. This wasn't a voting fee, but a tax that Massachusetts levied on all men over the age of nineteen. Thoreau had refused to pay it as a way of protesting his state's support of slavery in the United States.

It is not clear why Staples arrested Thoreau that particular day. Thoreau hadn't paid the tax for the past three years. Staples had repeatedly reminded him of the debt but issued no ultimatum until that summer day. Why then? One speculation is that Staples was about to retire and wanted to clear the books.

In any case, Thoreau spent the night in jail. The next day he learned that his Aunt Maria had paid his taxes. He told Staples he didn't want to leave his cell, but Staples made him go.

Concord residents expressed curiosity about Thoreau's decision to go to jail, so he explained his reasoning in a public lecture. Later he turned the lecture into an essay titled "Resistance to Civil Government" (later republished as "Civil Disobedience"). Thoreau argued that when one's conscience conflicts with the government's laws, one's duty is to obey one's conscience. The essay had a major impact on Leo Tolstoy and Mohandas Gandhi.

Animal Welfare

Thoreau hunted and fished as a boy, and when he lived at Walden Pond, he initially fished when he was very hungry. But he soon adopted a thoroughly vegetarian diet. He felt humans have some inner sense that they ought to refrain from eating meat—a sense that was faint but would prevail as our species evolved. Humans, he believed, will eventually recognize that every creature holds its life as dearly as we hold our own. Thoreau wasn't entirely consistent on this matter, however. He still supported hunting among boys as an activity that came naturally to them.

Over the years Thoreau learned a great deal about nature and provided considerable knowledge to distinguished Massachusetts scientists. He also killed some animals to provide them with specimens but came to feel this was wrong and stopped. One day a man asked him, "Don't you ever shoot a bird when you want to study it?" Thoreau replied, "Do you think that I should shoot you if I wanted to study you?"

For Thoreau, the issue was not only a moral one. He also opposed the study of dead specimens, as well as the study of animals in captivity, on scientific grounds. He believed we can learn more about animals by observing them living freely in their natural environment. In this respect he anticipated major twentieth-century ethologists such as Konrad Lorenz and Jane Goodall.

Trees

Thoreau loved trees. When Concord residents cut down an ancient elm, he felt that the town had lost a venerable part of itself. In fact, Thoreau held a personal funeral for the tree. As it lay on the ground, he gave a brief eulogy. If he felt his behavior was odd, he didn't say so. He merely noted that only a few people were near enough to hear him speak—the choppers and a few passersby. "The fathers of the town, the selectmen, the clergy were not there...The town clerk will not chronicle its fall."

At the same time, Thoreau recognized that his work as a surveyor contributed to the destruction of trees. He hoped new trees would replace the fallen ones, but he still felt guilty. As Walls says, "Long stretches of surveying always left him grouchy and snappish."

Later Years

In 1859, when Thoreau was forty-two years old, the abolitionist John Brown conducted his failed raid on Harpers Ferry, Virginia, and was tried for murder. Brown was widely denounced as a maniac, but Thoreau gave ringing public lectures in Brown's defense. As Walls says, Thoreau spoke out when no one else would.

Thoreau continued to take long walks in nature until he was forty-three, when he came down with tuberculosis. The illness lasted a year and a half, until his death at the age of forty-four. Until the end, Thoreau worked on his writings and kept his spirits up.

While he was bedridden, neighborhood children were among those to visit him. Bronson Alcott, who three years earlier had been appointed Concord's superintendent of schools, let classes out early so children could attend Thoreau's funeral. In his eulogy Emerson said, "The country knows not yet how great a son it has lost."

The Attitudes We Need

Fresh and Childlike Observation

In Thoreau's view, childhood is the precious time when we are most receptive to the miracle of nature. With fresh and keen senses, children experience animals, breezes, flowers—indeed, every aspect of nature they encounter—with wonder and delight.

Thoreau believed that adults, in contrast, perceive nature through society's conventional categories. Adults see what they expect to see. Little is new. Thoreau emphasized that scientists also view the natural world through conventional nomenclature and classifications, rendering their knowledge stale and dry.

Thoreau asked us to consider the child's discovery of fishes. "Was it the number of their fin-rays or their arrangement, or the place of the fish in some [scientific classification] system that made the boy dream of them?" No, it was their beauty and "a faint recognition of a living contemporary, a provoking mystery." Unfortunately, Thoreau said, children lose this sense of beauty and mystery as they grow up.

Our great task as adults, Thoreau believed, is to recapture the outlook of the child. He urged us to open ourselves to nature's sensations as if we were experiencing them for the first time, receiving her impressions just as they come to us. If we do this, nature will reveal her miraculous qualities directly to us, as she does to the child.

Thoreau recognized that his advice is difficult to follow. We might try to adopt a fresh, childlike outlook, but our adult mental habits are deeply ingrained. It's hard to get outside the customary ways of viewing things.

It's also difficult to adopt a fresh outlook because we value our accumulated knowledge. We don't want to be naive or ignorant. We take pride in being in the know.

Thoreau himself struggled to see the world anew, but he found it helpful to take walks or paddle his boat without any goal in mind—to let his focus wander with "a sauntering of the eye." His goal wasn't to search for objects or to analyze them, but to be taken by surprise.

If his journals are any indication, Thoreau's approach was quite successful. The journals are filled with unexpected observations, which are frequently described just as they occurred. While he was paddling his boat at sunrise, lilies suddenly unfolded before his eyes. "Fields of white blossom were opened before me, almost at a flash." When his boat bumps into some lilies, "I am struck by the splendid crimson-red of the underside." When the lilies close up at midday, Thoreau again gives his precise, unedited perception of the moment: "Looking toward the sun, I cannot see them, cannot distinguish lilies from the sun reflected from the pads."

As David Robinson emphasizes, Thoreau also learned that he could experience the world as fresh and new by taking walks at night and under moonlight. Sounds and scents were magnified; mists rose; the moon cast unusual shadows, creating eerie scenes. "On all sides," Thoreau wrote, "novelties present themselves."

Many of Thoreau's daytime journal entries are about birds, and even familiar species reveal new qualities. He spots a robin, a species he has associated with the village, but he now hears "an aboriginal wildness in his strain."

Similarly, Thoreau hears a flicker, whose chirp sounds monotonous. But Thoreau is surprised by the way the sound "enriches all the woods and fields! It seems to put a life into withered grass and leaves and bare twigs."

The bird that most powerfully stirred him was the wood thrush. The bird "launches forth one strain with all his heart and life and soul, of pure and unmatchable melody." Then the bird pauses and "launches forth another and another."

Thoreau was eager to explain why the thrush's song is so wonderful. It "is no opera music"; it is much simpler. But even when heard in the heat of the day,

> ... there is the liquid coolness of things that are just drawn from the bottom of springs.... Whenever a man hears it, he is young, and Nature is in her spring. Wherever he hears it, it is a new world and a free country, and the gates of heaven are not shut against him.

There is an attitude of reverence in Thoreau's writing. He frequently wrote about the way birds, breezes, and landscapes opened him to heaven, the immortal, and the eternal. Thoreau said such experiences were strongest in his youth, when his senses were keenest. When young, he experienced in nature such "divine, heavenly pleasure" that he felt he was in the hands of "superior powers."

Thoreau found some support for his emphasis on fresh perception in the writings of English art critic John Ruskin. Ruskin advocated artwork that abandoned prior knowledge of objects and depicted them just as they appeared. Painting gains power, Ruskin said, when the artist perceives the world through the "innocent eye," looking at things much as a child does. Ruskin's writing helped launch the Impressionist movement in painting, but Thoreau was dissatisfied with it. He felt that Ruskin focused so strongly on artistic renditions of nature that he ignored nature herself.

As mentioned, Thoreau learned a tremendous amount about nature and contributed to scientists' knowledge. Harvard even appointed him to give an exam in botany. But as his scientific expertise grew, he worried that his outlook was becoming hardened and narrow. He felt he was losing his open delight in nature. When a student wrote for advice, Thoreau told him, "It's only when we forget our learning that we begin to know."

In one journal passage, Thoreau hinted that it might be possible to *combine* childlike enthusiasm with scientific knowledge. He praised an old book on plants because, while scientifically sound, it presented plants with the joy of a "child who has just seen a flower for the first time and comes running in with it to his friends." But if we must choose between scientific expertise and childhood enthusiasm, Thoreau favored the latter.

Unhurried Living

To perceive the world freshly, Thoreau believed, we cannot be in a rush. On his long walks and boat outings, he liked to meander along, feeling nature's rhythms. He abandoned destinations and schedules, for he wanted to be open to what was happening in the present moment. In this way, he felt he could perceive things as they really are.

When Thoreau came across something interesting, he sometimes sat or stood still for a long time. For example, Thoreau spotted some frogs in a pond, who then disappeared from sight. Thoreau didn't leave, but continued to sit beside the pond, and after a while they poked their noses out of the water and curiously looked at him. Eventually they came hopping up beside him and allowed him to scratch their noses with his finger.

To many people, Thoreau appeared to spend hour upon hour doing nothing at all—at least nothing productive. A farmer, Mr. Murray, told a writer how he saw Thoreau standing beside an old mud pond all day long: "He wasn't doin' nothin' but just standing there—looking at that pond." Finally, Mr. Murray asked Thoreau what he was doing, and Thoreau told him he was studying the habits of the bullfrog. "And there that darned fool had been standin'—the livelong day—a-studyin'—the habits—of the *bull*-frog!"

Children took a different view. One girl, who saw Thoreau standing all day at the edge of a river, was careful not to disturb him. At suppertime, he went to her house and reported that he had watched a duck teach her newborns about the river. The girl said, "While we ate our suppers there in the kitchen, he told us the most wonderful stories you ever heard about those ducks."

Thoreau recognized that his wish to spend leisurely time in nature put him at odds with the work ethic of the adult society. And he was irritated by criticism of his behavior. In *Walden* he wrote,

> If a man walks in the woods for the love of them half of each day, he is in danger of being regarded as a loafer; but if he spends his whole day as a specula-tor, shearing off those woods and making earth bald before her time, he is esteemed as an industrious and enterprising citizen.

At One with Nature

A few weeks after Thoreau moved to Walden Pond, he sat in his house during a gentle rain and felt lonely. He worried that he might need more human companion-ship. Then he experienced an unexpected kinship with nature. He looked outside his house and felt "an infinite and unaccountable friendliness all at once like an atmo-sphere sustaining me." He said,

> Every little pine needle expanded and swelled with sympathy and befriended me. I was...distinctly made aware of the presence of something kindred to me.

This kind of writing has come under sharp criticism. In the language of scientists, Thoreau had fallen prey to animism or anthropomorphism; he was projecting his own emotions—his wish for friendship—onto imper-sonal nature. In literary circles, such projections come under the heading of "the pathetic fallacy."

Thoreau recognized that his perceptions would sound strange to the conventional ear. But he defended them. He believed that if we open ourselves fully to nature, we will find that it has moods, just like we do. This is because, Thoreau felt, there is no sharp division between us and the rest of nature. We participate in the underlying unity of life. As he explained, "Shall I not have intelligence with the earth? Am I not partly leaves and vegetable mould myself?"

Was Thoreau correct? Some of his specific perceptions, such as the friendliness of pine needles, may have been the product of his imagination. At the same time, Thoreau was generally on the right track. Modern biologists have been amazed by the unity of life. For example, biologists have discovered that all life-forms use the same genetic code and create proteins out of the same amino acids. Thoreau didn't have this information, of course. So he called attention to the unity of life through other thoughts and observations. For example:

The humblest fungus betrays a life akin to my own.

There is a calmness of the lake...So it is with us.

It is not merely crow calling to crow, for it speaks to me too. I am part of one

great creature with him; if he has a voice, I have ears.

Feeling at one with nature, Thoreau believed we should honor other animals as much as we honor our own kind. Thoreau saved his most passionate comments for the muskrat caught in a trap. "Shall we not have sympathy with the muskrat which gnaws its third leg

off…appreciating its majestic pains and its heroic vir-
tue?" Thoreau said the brave muskrat should be celebrated
in our religious ceremonies. Praise for nonhuman animals
should be equal to that of humans.

Getting into the Seasons

Thoreau urged us to develop our feelings of oneness with
nature by immersing ourselves in her seasons. Each sea-
son has its distinctive mood, and we need to become at
one with it. Spring is the time to be cheerful like the
birds; summer is a time to relax and enjoy nature's bounty
and sweetness. Autumn is for reflection, winter for solidi-
fying and perfecting our thoughts.

Thoreau emphasized that we become estranged from
nature by spending so much time indoors. We attempt to
insulate ourselves from the heat, winds, cold, and snow,
but our health suffers. We might think we "are not well
in spring, or summer, or autumn, or winter" but it is only
because we "are not well in them." We need to remember
that we are part of nature. Our health thrives when we
are in tune with her.

Although Thoreau found something precious in
every aspect of nature, he took special delight in birdsong
and morning light. Indeed, he believed that there was
no more important question than, "How is it that light
comes into the soul?" And he concluded his great essay,
"Walking," with words on sunlight. He hoped we would
walk in nature "till one day the sun shall shine more
brightly than ever he has done, shall perchance shine
into our minds and hearts, and light up our whole lives."

~

A Sample of Thoreau Quotes

Fresh Perception and Wonder

"To perceive freshly, with fresh senses, is to be inspired."

"The child plucks its first flower with an insight into its beauty and significance which the subsequent botanist never retains."

"If you would be wise, learn science and then forget it."

"Take an original and unprejudiced view of Nature, letting her make what impressions she will on you, as the first men, and all children and natural men still do."

"Go not to the object; let it come to you."

"Wisdom does not inspect, but beholds."

"Experience is in the fingers and head. The heart is inexperienced."

"It is only necessary to behold thus the least fact or phenomenon a hair's breadth aside from the habitual path or routine, to be overcome, enchanted."

"All the phenomena of nature need to be seen from the point of view of wonder and awe, like lightning."

Nature

"Bathe in all the tides of nature ... For all Nature is doing her best each moment to make us well."

"I hear the universal cock-crowing with surprise and pleasure, as if I never heard it before. What a tough fellow! How native to the earth!"

"The sound of the crickets at dawn after these first sultry nights seems like the dreaming of the earth still continued into daylight."

"The wood thrush is a more modern philosopher than Plato and Aristotle. They are now a dogma, but he preaches the doctrine of this hour."

"Nowadays almost all man's improvements, so called, as the building of houses and the cutting down of the forest and of all large trees, simply deform the landscape, and make it more and more tame and cheap."

On fishes whose migration is blocked by a dam: "Who hears the fishes when they cry?"

"I love even to see the domestic animals reassert their native rights—any evidence that they have not wholly lost their original wild habits and vigor; as when my neighbor's cow breaks out of her pasture early in the spring and boldly swims the river . . ."

"Where the most wonderful wild-flowers grow, there man's spirit is fed, and poets grow."

Society

"Here is this vast, savage, mother of ours, Nature, lying all around, with such beauty, and such affection for her children, as the leopard; and yet we are so early weaned from her breast to society, to that culture which is exclusively an interaction of man on man, a sort of breeding in and in . . ."

"In society, in the best institutions of men, it is easy to detect a certain precocity. When we should still be growing children, we are already little men."

"What does education do!—It makes a straight-cut ditch of a free, meandering brook."

"I hate museums . . . They are dead nature collected by dead men."

"How deep the ruts of tradition and conformity."

"It is possible for a man wholly to disappear and be merged in his manners."

When injustice reins, "Let your life be a counter friction to stop the machine."

⤞ 2 ⤝

Albert Einstein

·······

*Contemplating the Wonder
and Mystery of the Universe*

*[Einstein was] a man of humility and profound sim-
plicity who preserved the wide-eyed wonder of a child.*
                                        —Banesh Hoffmann

The psychoanalyst Erik Erikson referred to Albert
Einstein as "the victorious child," as one who "suc-
ceeded in saving the child in himself." Einstein would
have agreed. He spoke about childhood as something
precious, full of curiosity and wonder, which runs up
against an "education-machine" that crushes it with rigid
discipline and mind-numbing instruction. Einstein felt
that he was unusual because he was able to maintain the
spirit of childhood throughout his life, and this spirit was
the wellspring of his amazing creativity. Let us review his
life and see how this occurred.

Early Years

Albert Einstein (1879–1955) grew up in Munich, Germany. His father Hermann was in the electrical supply business, and his mother Pauline was a homemaker with a cultured background and a strong interest in music.

Albert's early language development was slow. He didn't speak during his first three years of life, and his family was worried that he was intellectually backward. Once he did begin speaking, he had a habit of formulating sentences silently, moving his lips, before coming out with the words. This behavior lasted until he was seven years old.

Socially, he was rather isolated. He didn't play much with other children, preferring activities such as block building, working on jigsaw puzzles, and making houses of cards. His main friend was his sister Maja, who was a year younger.

Outwardly, then, Albert appeared to be a slowly developing, solitary child. But beneath the surface was a strong curiosity and sense of wonder. In his "Autobiographical Notes," he told how, at age four or five,

> my father showed me a compass. That this needle behaved in such a determined way did not at all fit into the nature of events...I can still remember—or at least believe I can remember—that this experience made a deep and lasting impression on me. Something deeply hidden had to be behind things...

When he was five years old, his parents enrolled him in a nearby Catholic school. Although they were Jewish, they weren't very religious and believed that the school was a good one. Albert, however, didn't like the emphasis on discipline and rote learning. He wanted to take the time to think about problems for himself rather than immediately accepting the "right" answers.

Nor did Albert strike the school as a good student. When his father asked the headmaster about the kind of future career he foresaw for Albert, the headmaster said the question was irrelevant because Albert would never be successful at anything.

When Albert was ten, the family enrolled him in a traditional German school called a gymnasium. Like his first school, this one emphasized rote learning, what Einstein later called the "dull, mechanized method of teaching." Making matters worse, the teachers at the gymnasium adopted a militaristic, drill sergeant approach which was especially upsetting to him. As one of Einstein's biographers, Banesh Hoffmann said,

> Even as a child, Albert recoiled instinctively from coercion. He shuddered at the sight and sound of military parades. While other children looked forward eagerly to the time when they too could don uniforms, he loathed the very thought of marching in mindless unison to the empty beat of a drum.

In school, Albert kept his anger over the instruction to himself and earned moderately good grades. To an extent, his early difficulty with language seemed to persist; he performed most poorly on subjects that required him to remember words and verbal texts. In addition, Albert's slow way of thinking irritated some of his teachers. A teacher of Greek once became so exasperated that he burst out that Albert would never amount to anything.

Eagerly Learning Outside School

Albert's schoolwork was better in math and science, but his abilities in these areas really blossomed outside school. His Uncle Jakob, an engineer, introduced him to concepts in mathematics, and Albert was fascinated. Jakob posed increasingly difficult problems, and Albert consistently solved them.

At the age of twelve he came upon a little book on Euclidean geometry. It filled him with as much wonder as the compass did when was younger. He marveled how ideas could be proved with such clarity and certainty.

At this time, a young medical student named Max Talmey visited the Einstein family for dinner on Thursdays. It was the practice of many European families to help financially strapped students get a good meal. Talmey introduced Albert to popular science books, and Albert found them riveting.

Religious Crisis

The science books also caused Albert to reevaluate his earlier religious beliefs. Even though his parents weren't religious, the law required that he receive instruction in his parents' faith at home. Albert had become enthusiastic about Judaism and believed in the Bible. Then the science books convinced him that many biblical stories couldn't be true. His faith was shaken. Albert became suspicious of all authority. Indeed, he felt that the state and the schools were intentionally deceiving young people.

Unable to believe in religion, Albert might have decided to focus on his own personal desires and ambitions. But he did not. He still wanted to understand something much larger than himself, and he turned to the scientific exploration of the natural world. As he wrote in his "Autobiographical Notes,"

> Out there was this huge world, which exists independently of us as human beings and which stands before us like a great, eternal riddle, at least partially accessible to our inspection and thinking.

The Violin

From the ages of six to fourteen, Albert took violin lessons. Einstein later wrote that he "had no luck with my teachers for whom music did not transcend mechanical practicing. I really began to learn only when I was about 13 years old, mainly after I had fallen in love with Mozart's sonatas." Inspired to express the grace of the sonatas, he worked to improve his technique. This he did largely on his own. Einstein said, "I believe, on the whole, that love is a better teacher than a sense of duty—with me, at least, it certainly was." Einstein loved the violin so much that he played it all his life.

Dropout and Failure

When Albert was fifteen, he went through a difficult period. His parents and sister moved to Italy so his father could pursue brighter business prospects. Albert's parents wanted him to complete his final three years at the gymnasium, so they left him in Munich to live in a boardinghouse under the supervision of a relative. Albert missed his family and became very depressed.

After six months, he figured out a way to leave school and rejoin his family. He persuaded a doctor to write a note that said he was suffering from a nervous disorder.

Ironically, when he showed the note to the principal, he was told the note was unnecessary because he was being expelled. The reason, the principal said, was that Albert had irritated a teacher by sitting in the back row of the class with a smile, violating "the feeling of respect which a teacher needs from a class."

Albert felt an increasingly strong need to free himself from the dominant culture and institutions. When he rejoined his family in Italy, he told them he had decided to renounce his German citizenship and his Jewish faith. But he also reassured his parents that he was still committed to his education. With their support, he spent a year touring Italy, especially enjoying the museums. Then he studied for and took the entrance exams at the Polytechnic Institute in Zurich.

Albert failed. He did exceptionally well in math and science, but he did not perform well in history, languages, and literature. This setback could have ended his scientific future, but Albert ran into a bit of unexpected luck.

A Year at a Child-Centered School

The head of the Polytechnic Institute saw the young man's potential and told Albert's family that he might benefit from a year in a secondary school in the small Swiss town of Aarau. The family agreed and arranged for Albert to live with the family of the school's principal, Jost Winteler.

The school followed the principles of Johann Heinrich Pestalozzi, who believed education should be nurturing and enjoyable. Pestalozzi said, "Learning is not worth a penny if courage and joy are lost along the way." Inspired by the writings of Jean-Jacques Rousseau, Pestalozzi wanted teachers to be attuned to children's natural ways of growing and learning.

Like Rousseau, Pestalozzi distrusted book learning; he thought it teaches children to talk about matters they know nothing about. Instead of an early focus on reading, he wanted children to first develop their powers of observation of real objects.

Albert soon became fond of the principal's family and was very happy at the school. Never comfortable with verbal learning, he appreciated the school's encouragement to apprehend life visually and through the senses. He also loved the relaxed atmosphere and students' freedom to think for themselves.

He especially enjoyed long walks in the mountains—sometimes alone, sometimes with classmates. The breathtaking scenery and beauty had a powerful effect on him. One of his biographers, Antonina Vallentin, who knew Einstein personally, wrote that, "Nature gave him self-confidence as no human being could have done." Vallentin didn't explain *how* nature gave him self-confidence, but perhaps it made him feel good to be alive and part of a wonderful world. Perhaps the beauty affirmed his decision to understand nature's laws. Nature's magical wonder might have made the effort seem eminently worthwhile.

Albert continued to think about physics, especially about electricity and light, and it was during this time (when he was sixteen) that he engaged in his first "thought experiment." He asked himself what a beam of light would look like to someone keeping pace with it. Paradoxically, the beam would appear to be at rest, whereas to an observer standing still the beam's speed would be nothing but a flash. Einstein later wrote that this paradox formed the germ of his theory of special relativity.

The Polytechnic Institute

At the end of a year at the Swiss school, he received the diploma that would enable him to begin studies at the Polytechnic Institute in Zurich. He signed up for a program that would lead to a teaching degree but soon found himself absorbed in joyful work in physics labs. He frequently skipped lectures, but a classmate, Marcel Grossmann, lent him lecture notes that helped him pass the graduation exams.

The exams, however, took an emotional toll. He hated that he was forced to cram all kinds of material into his mind, whether he liked it or not. "This coercion," he wrote, "had such a deterring effect [upon me] that, after I had passed the final examination, I found the consideration of any scientific problems distasteful to me for an entire year."

Einstein added that,

It is, in fact, nothing short of a miracle that the modern methods of instruction have not yet entirely strangled the holy curiosity of inquiry; for this delicate little plant, aside from stimulation, stands mainly in need of freedom; without this it goes to wreck and ruin without fail.

Job Search

Einstein's interest in physics did revive, but he couldn't find a university job. He wrote to many physicists, offering his services as an assistant, but there were no takers. Einstein said he was rebuffed because he wasn't "in the good graces of any of my former teachers," who disliked his independent attitude. As the head of the Polytechnic

Institute once told him, "You're a clever fellow! But you have one fault. You won't let anyone tell you a thing."

In 1901, at the age of twenty-one, Einstein tried a series of temporary teaching and tutoring jobs, but barely made enough money to live on. He submitted a research paper to the University of Zurich, which he hoped would satisfy the dissertation requirement for a PhD, but it was rejected.

In 1902 his situation improved. He landed a job as a patent clerk in Bern, which gave him a stable, if modest, income. Moreover, it gave him time to carry out his first great work.

"The Olympia Academy"

Einstein moved to Bern a few months before the job at the patent office began, and to make ends meet, he put an advertisement in a newspaper to offer tutoring in physics. A young philosophy student named Maurice Solovine answered the ad and met with Einstein in his apartment. The young men got into an exciting two-hour discussion of philosophy and physics, after which Einstein accompanied Solovine out onto the sidewalk, where they continued their discussion for another half hour. Einstein didn't charge Solovine any money, and soon three others joined the two for regular discussions of physics, philosophy, and prospects for a better society. Among the writers they read was Ernst Mach, who speculated about relativity in physics.

The group joking called itself "The Olympia Academy." All the members were roughly Einstein's age and either completing graduate studies or beginning their careers. None had any money. Einstein served his friends coffee and the light meals he could afford. Sometimes a few of the friends took long walks on the mountainside, thrilling at the sunrises and sunsets.

Einstein loved these intellectual discussions, and they provided vital support as he formulated his revolutionary ideas. Near the end of his life, he wrote a letter to Solovine to express the group's importance. Addressed "To the Immortal Olympia Academy," Einstein wrote: "In your brief and active existence, you took a childlike joy in all that was clear and intelligent... Your bright and life-giving light still shines on our life's lonely path."

It is not surprising that Einstein praised the group's "childlike" attitude. As briefly mentioned at the beginning of this chapter, Einstein assigned special importance to children's thinking. Solovine said that when Einstein was formulating his ideas, he frequently talked about his observations of how children think about space and time. Solovine did not specify precisely what childhood thoughts impressed Einstein, and I have not been able to find this out. I would love to know. What we do know is that Einstein prized children's curiosity and found that children ask more original questions than adults.

In 1903, Einstein married Mileva Marić, who was also studying physics at the Polytechnic Institute. They were in love and had children, but Einstein didn't give his family the time he felt it deserved. When not at work at the patent office, Einstein was engrossed in the world of ideas, particularly in theoretical physics. Sometimes Mileva sat in on discussions of the Olympia Academy, but she didn't say much.

One member of the discussion group, Michele Besso, served as a private sounding board for Einstein's emerging ideas on the theory relativity. As Einstein told Besso the problems with which he was struggling, Besso listened thoughtfully and asked penetrating questions. Sometimes Besso purposely challenged Einstein's thinking, but it was always to help Einstein clarify his thoughts. Through it all, Besso was consistently enthusiastic. In Einstein's first 1905 paper on special relativity, there were no references to other physicists—only a note thanking Besso.

Relativity

The year 1905 is called Einstein's "Year of Miracles." It was when he published two papers introducing his first theory of relativity. Actually, these were only the last two of five papers he published that year, and all were of enormous theoretical importance. But his papers on relativity, above all, announced a new way of seeing the world.

In classic Newtonian physics, there is a single fixed system for measuring all events. Einstein, however, observed that measurements differ for an observer in motion compared to an observer who is stationary. Time measurements are relative.

Hearing about "the theory of relativity," people have sometimes inferred that Einstein wanted to show that everything is subjective, that there are no absolutes in physics. But this wasn't Einstein's goal. He felt that even though observers might measure events differently, there were aspects of physics that are constant. The work of James Clerk Maxwell and others led Einstein to postulate that one constant in the universe is the speed of light. So the problem became: if people measure events differently depending on whether they are at rest or in motion, why will observers always measure the speed of light as the same?

Einstein wrestled mightily with the problem. To solve it, he made a proposal that defied common sense. Time, he ventured, goes more slowly for a person in motion. Physicists call this "time dilation." In ordinary life, we don't travel fast enough to notice time dilation, but Einstein predicted that it would be perceptible at very high speeds. Even clocks will be found to have moved more slowly. Following the suggestions of a few others, Einstein speculated that space also shrinks with movement. With this new view of both time and space as varying, Einstein showed why the speed of light will always be measured as the same.

When he published his theory, he was twenty-six years old, and he had developed a satisfying answer to a question that had troubled him since the age of sixteen. That is, how would a beam of light appear to someone chasing it at the same amazing speed as the light? Part of the answer is that it's impossible to travel that fast, for reasons explained in aspects of his theory that I won't cover. But for someone traveling *close to* the speed of light, light would still appear to travel at the same amazing speed. As physicist Michio Kaku says, if we somehow could ride a vehicle at almost the speed of light, the light would appear to flash away from us. The speed of light is constant, and the concepts of time dilation and space dilation explain why this is so.

Einstein's 1905 theory of relativity was limited to special cases. It compared observers at rest with observers in motion—but only when the motion is *uniform*. Because his 1905 theory applied only to special cases, the theory became known as the *special theory of relativity*.

Despite this limitation, the theory revolutionized physics. Its development required not only genius but superhuman effort. When Einstein finished his first paper on special relativity, he physically collapsed from exhaustion. It took him two weeks to recover. He then worked on his second paper on special relativity, also published in 1905, which took steps toward his famous equation E = mc2.

Einstein's sister Maja reported that his 1905 papers received sparse attention and he was disappointed. But one physicist immediately saw the importance of Einstein's first paper on relativity, and within two months he had told others to pay attention to it. Luckily for Einstein, this physicist was the esteemed Max Planck.

Einstein's theory—especially the concept of time dilation—remained controversial, but when physicists were finally able to test the concept experimentally in 1938, the results supported it. Today's satellite-based GPS systems rely on the concept of time dilation for their calculations.

The sidebar presents a timeline of major events in Einstein's professional life from 1901 to 1921. I have already mentioned some of these up to 1905. After 1905, Einstein's greatest accomplishment—and arguably his most amazing achievement—was *the general theory of relativity*.

∽

Timeline 1901 to 1921

1901 Submits a paper to the University of Zurich to satisfy requirement for a PhD, but the paper is rejected.

1902 The "Olympia Academy" (the stimulating discussion group Einstein was a part of) begins.

1902 Starts work in Swiss patent office.

1905 Einstein's "Year of Miracles." He publishes five groundbreaking papers, the last two on the special theory of relativity.

1905   Submits the second of the papers, on molecules, to the University of Zurich for his PhD dissertation. It is rejected as too short. Einstein promptly adds a single sentence and resubmits it. It is accepted.

1906   Einstein receives his PhD from the University of Zurich.

1907   Publishes his famous $E = mc^2$ formula, expressing the interchangeable nature of mass and energy.

1907   Begins work on the general theory of relativity.

1909   Leaves the patent office to assume his first full-time paid faculty position at the University of Zurich.

1915   Finds that his general theory of relativity predicts the orbit of Mercury—something Newtonian physics couldn't do. Reports result to the Prussian Academy of Sciences on November 18.

1915   Presents his completed theory in November 25 lecture to the Prussian Academy.

1916   Publishes the first full account of general relativity in a small book titled *The Foundation of the Generalized Theory of Relativity*.

1919   British astronomer Frank Dyson leads two expeditions to examine solar eclipses. When light refractions support the general theory of relativity, England buzzes with the news, and Einstein becomes world-famous.

1921   Einstein is awarded the Nobel Prize for his first 1905 paper, which suggested that light can take the form of both particles and waves.

The General Theory of Relativity

Einstein's 1905 papers on special relativity not only were restricted to uniform motion; they also said nothing about an enormously important variable in physics, the force of gravity. Einstein wanted to develop a broader theory, a general theory of relativity, that would account for variations in motion and for gravity as well. He began this work in 1907.

Progress on the theory was slow and came in fits and starts. Einstein received mathematical assistance from Marcel Grossmann—the same man who gave Einstein his lecture notes in graduate school—but minor errors cost him at least two years of extra work. Einstein said the entire effort included "years of anxious searching in the dark, with their intense longing, their alternations of confidence and exhaustion."

To account for both gravity and motion in general, Einstein conceived of the radical idea of curved space-time. In this conception, objects do not move toward each other because of Newton's mysterious gravitational pull. They move according to their effect on space-time, like bowling balls moving toward the center of a trampoline. Einstein had developed a new conception of the universe.

In 1915, when he was in the final stages of his work, he continued to confront mathematical obstacles. He told a famous mathematician, David Hilbert, about the problems, and Hilbert independently tried to figure out the mathematical equations that would complete Einstein's theory. Einstein knew about Hilbert's efforts, and he didn't want to be scooped by Hilbert. But it is unlikely that competition with Hilbert motivated Einstein to work so hard. Einstein didn't pour himself into his work to gain social recognition, but to catch glimpses of the "sublimity and marvelous order" in nature. His efforts were more like those of a pilgrim on a spiritual quest. He said the exhausting work of theoretical physics requires this kind of passion, which comes "straight from the heart."

Late in 1915, Einstein decided to see if his mathematical revisions were on the right track. He decided to see if his theory could predict the orbit of the planet Mercury. This was something Newtonian physics couldn't do and something Einstein's own previous formulations had failed to do. The new outcome was positive: his revisions did, indeed, predict Mercury's orbit. Einstein was beside himself with joy.

Einstein then discarded some cumbersome concepts and presented his theory to the Prussian Academy of Sciences on November 25, 1915. In his biography of Einstein, Banesh Hoffmann, himself an accomplished physicist, described Einstein's theory as possessing "majestic simplicity" and "indescribable beauty."

A few scholars have debated whether Einstein or Hilbert was the first to announce the equations that completed the theory. In a careful review of the debate, Walter Isaacson says that Einstein was probably the first to publish the full version of the equations. Moreover, Hilbert credited Einstein as being the sole author of the general theory of relativity.

In 1919 a British expedition found that two eclipses also supported Einstein's predictions. This outcome was widely reported in the news and made Einstein a world-famous figure.

Nobel Prize

In 1921, Einstein won the Nobel Prize in Physics. Einstein had been nominated nine times before he finally received the award. Why the delay? Anti-Semitism played a role. In addition, many scientists remained skeptical of Einstein's relativity theories.

When Einstein finally received the prize, it wasn't for either theory of relativity. The prize was awarded for Einstein's first 1905 paper, which suggested that light can take the form of both particles and waves—a proposal that helped initiate quantum theory. Like relativity, quantum theory was revolutionary, but it was less theoretical. It was the subject of much more experimental research.

"God Does Not Play Dice"

Einstein's 1905 contribution to quantum theory was ironic because he later became frustrated with the theory. Quantum theory deals with physics on the small scale of atomic and subatomic particles and is probabilistic; its equations provide statistical predictions of events that are likely, but not certain, to occur. Einstein searched for certainty. He sought universal laws that would reveal nature's perfect and beautiful harmony. He had made progress on the large scale of the solar system, but on the small atomic scale, quantum theory reigned. Einstein expressed his resistance to quantum theory's probabilistic approach in his famous statement, "God does not play dice."

After completing his general theory of relativity, Einstein tried to develop a unified field theory that would unite physics on both scales, large and small, into a single set of laws. He spent the rest of his life on this task, but he couldn't accomplish it.

A Stranger in Public Society

The British expedition of 1919 made Einstein famous, but the Einstein who burst onto the world stage was no polished diplomat. Even at the most formal occasions, he usually appeared disheveled, his hair unruly and wearing an oft-mended sweater and sandals.

One day Einstein paid a visit to a former teacher who was the only one who had encouraged students to think for themselves. Einstein wanted to express his appreciation. But when he arrived at the elderly teacher's door, the teacher didn't recognize him. In fact, Einstein was dressed so shabbily that the teacher assumed Einstein was a beggar and ordered his maid to send him away.

Einstein disliked large gatherings, and even among a small group of acquaintances he was prone to fall into strange absences. It is likely that his thoughts drifted to scientific problems, which were always on his mind. Einstein's friend Vallentin said,

> Suddenly he would fall silent and stop listening to you... He might appear lost to us for a long time, and then return to us as if he had never realized his absence... His presence among us was only a temporary loan.

Einstein did have friends. He also married twice and had children. But he basically considered himself a loner. And his wish to withdraw from others, he wrote in 1930, was increasing with age. He recognized that his detachment came at an emotional cost, but he said it also freed him from the conventional outlooks on which more sociable people depend. Moreover, his mental absences in social gatherings, in which he turned inward, were probably related to his capacity to invest his whole being in deep thought.

Vallentin observed a contradiction with respect to Einstein's social isolation. Although he was often inaccessible to others, he was also sympathetic toward fellow humans and thought about social problems. He was a staunch advocate of world peace, socialism, freedom of thought, the formation of Israel, and the rights of African Americans. He was sympathetic toward animals and increasingly adhered to a vegetarian diet. He thought about the meaning of life and concluded that "Only a life lived for others is a life worthwhile."

In his daily life, there was one group of people with whom Einstein felt at home: children. He loved being around them and took delight in their innocent questioning. Vallentin said,

> He loves their naivete, still unaffected by conventional restraints, their impetuous questions, and their lack of embarrassment about gaps they reveal in their knowledge. Above all Einstein shares their laughter and that mysterious sense of humor that makes grown-ups exclaim: "What on earth are they laughing about!"

The Power of Childhood

People have speculated on the source of Einstein's remarkable achievements. How could he come up with such revolutionary theories? Some people looked for an explanation in his brain. After he died, several autopsies were performed, but nothing remarkable was found.

Autopsies, however, are not very sensitive assessment instruments with respect to intellectual capacities, so the disappointing results shouldn't be taken too seriously. Certainly Einstein had great intellectual abilities.

Beyond his intelligence, we need to consider personality traits that contributed to his achievements. He was able to lose himself in deep thought, and he also had a capacity for tremendously hard work.

Erik Erikson suggested, in addition, that Einstein was so creative because he retained the playfulness of childhood. Just as he played with blocks and cards when he was young, he played with images and ideas as a scientist, as in his thought experiments.

But Einstein himself talked relatively little about play. Instead, he emphasized the power of curiosity. As he once said, "I have no special gift—I am only passionately curious." And the source of this intense curiosity, he believed, is childhood as well. He said,

> There is such a thing as a passionate desire to understand, just as there is a passionate love for music. This passion is common with children, but it usually vanishes as they grow up. Without it, there would be no natural science and no mathematics.

Einstein felt that he, even more than most other scientists, had retained this childhood curiosity. He once joked that because his early development was so slow, he kept asking the questions that children ask.

Einstein believed that in dedicated scientists, curiosity is mixed with two other emotions: awe and a sense of mystery.

Scientists are filled with awe at the amazing harmony of nature's laws. As Einstein said, "Everyone who is seriously involved in the pursuit of science becomes convinced that a spirit is manifest in the laws of the Universe—a spirit vastly superior to that of man." And we humans, Einstein added, can comprehend nature's magnificent structure only imperfectly; we can only catch glimpses of it. We therefore face a great mystery.

Einstein said that this sense of mystery is at the heart of religion, the arts, science—and childhood. Einstein expressed this view in a letter to a friend, a psychiatrist by profession, which I have printed as an epigraph at the beginning of this book. Einstein wrote, "People like you and me...do not grow old no matter how long we live. What I mean is we never cease to stand like curious children before the great Mystery into which we are born."

↳ 3 ↲

Charlotte Brontë

·······

*Childhood Play Fuels
a Novelist's Imagination*

> This little light of mine,
> I'm gonna let it shine.
> Let it shine, let it shine, let it shine.
>
> —Gospel song

Beginning in early childhood, Charlotte Brontë experienced the deaths of several family members. In her struggles against the ensuing depression, she found pleasure in nature's beauty and the adventures of her vivid imagination. She developed her imagination through make-believe play with her siblings as a child, and they continued their play into their early twenties. Whether collaborating with her siblings or working alone, Charlotte created exciting dramas, stories, and poems. These creative activities provided relief from her suffering and led to great works of fiction.

Early Childhood

Charlotte Brontë (1816–1855) was born in Thornton, England. When she turned four, her family moved to the nearby village of Haworth, which became her lifelong home. Charlotte was a middle child, with two older sisters and three younger siblings. All were close in age.

After the move to Haworth, Charlotte's mother became ill and was soon bedridden. In her nineteenth-century biography of Brontë, Elizabeth Gaskell described the mother's ailment as an "internal cancer." The mother had been a cheerful and pious woman before her illness and tried to maintain a positive attitude, but she didn't see much of her children while she was bedridden. The sidebar lists the ages of the children when their mother took to her bed.

∾

The Brontë Siblings

Ages of the Brontë children when their mother became bedridden.

Maria	6
Elizabeth	5
Charlotte	4
Branwell	3
Emily	2
Anne	1

Charlotte's father, who had come to England from Ireland, was a bookish Anglican clergyman. He liked to tell his children his political opinions, but he was otherwise distant from them, spending most of his time alone in his study or with his wife. The children ate their meals apart from their parents.

When their mother became ill, an aunt—"Aunt Branwell"—joined the household. She, too, seems to have been emotionally distant from the youngsters. The family lived in an isolated house in a rural area, and the children had practically no contact with others their own age.

In this bleak and secluded household, the children bonded tightly together. Maria, the oldest—only six when their mother became ill—tried to keep the other children's spirits up. She led her siblings on walks on the moors— vast, wild land where heather bloomed and winds howled. Their mother's nurse later told Gaskell how she watched the six children walking "hand-in-hand," the older ones "taking thoughtful care for the toddling wee things." Maria also read the children newspaper articles and encouraged them to join together in games of make-believe.

Their mother died when Charlotte was five. Maria, who was then seven, continued to enliven the other children by organizing walks and make-believe play, and by reading to them.

The father and aunt taught the children some reading and writing, and the father continued to tutor his son Branwell at home for several years. Three years after his wife's death, he sent his daughters to a residential school to help prepare them for the vocations open to women— teaching or work as a governess.

A Miserable School

The school, Cowan Bridge, was like something out of a Dickens novel. All learning was by rote, and discipline was harsh. The buildings were cold and damp. The food was disgusting. One former student remembered grease from a dirty copper pot swimming on the top of the girls' warm milk. Children frequently went hungry rather than eat the rancid food. Some children came down with typhus and other illnesses. After a year at the school, Charlotte's two older sisters, Elizabeth and Maria, developed pneumonia. They were sent home and soon died. They were ten and eleven years old.

The deaths devastated Charlotte and her three younger siblings. Incredibly, Mr. Brontë sent Charlotte and Emily back to the school, but he brought them home in a month, when the school's conditions threatened their health as well.

Heartbroken and barely nine years old, Charlotte assumed the role of nurturing older sister to her siblings. Charlotte also performed numerous household chores. She cleaned rooms, ran errands, helped with the cooking, and mended clothes—all the while keeping an eye on the younger ones.

The only good news at this time was the addition to the household of a fifty-three-year-old servant named Tabitha Aykroyd. Tabby, as the children called her, was an old-fashioned, gruff woman, whose grandmotherly presence provided some comfort to them. Tabby's main task was cooking, and she wasn't good at it, but the children developed affection for her.

For the next five years, the children received formal instruction at home. Mr. Brontë taught Branwell Greek, Latin, history, and geography. He taught a few school subjects to the girls, but their instruction came largely from their aunt, who taught them homemaking skills and reading in English and French. In addition, the children took painting and drawing lessons from a local artist.

But to a considerable extent, the children took charge of their own education.

Exciting Books and Make-Believe Play

Their father gave them free access to his library, and the children eagerly explored it. They read books such as *Gulliver's Travels*, *The Arabian Nights*, *Aesop's Fables*, and the Bible, as well as works on history and poetry. Even the poems of Lord Byron, considered so scandalous for his thoughts on love and sex, were available to them, and they read him.

The children also resumed make-believe play. A key event occurred when Charlotte was ten. Mr. Brontë brought Branwell a box of wooden toy soldiers, which he left beside Branwell's bed during the night. The next morning Branwell took the soldiers to the girls' bedroom. Charlotte later recalled that,

> Emily and I jumped out of bed and I snatched up one and exclaimed, "This is the Duke of Wellington. This shall be the Duke!" When I said this, Emily likewise took one and said it should be hers; when Anne came down, she said one should be hers...Emily's was a grave looking fellow, and we called him "Gravey"...Branwell chose his, and called him "Buonaparte."

With these toys the children began creating elaborate dramas taking place on imaginary islands. They often worked in pairs. Charlotte and Branwell wove tales about an African kingdom named Angria; Emily and Anne created works about a land they called Gondal. Charlotte's favorite figure, the Duke of Wellington, was a real political figure whom she embellished. After a while, her attention turned to his fictitious son, the Duke of Zamorna. One of Brontë's biographers, Claire Harman, described this duke as "scandalous and ruthless, with dark secrets from his past suddenly revealed, mistresses and bastards discovered everywhere." The children's works also included fairies and genies with great magical powers.

As the children moved into their teen years, they increasingly put their creations into written form. They wrote plays, tales, letters, and poems. Some works were pieces for imaginary young people's magazines. Charlotte did the most writing. She wrote in tiny script, perhaps trying to mimic book print. The tiny print also might have been an attempt to keep the stories secret, for the works were all intended only for themselves.

The children illustrated their fantasy productions with their drawings. Charlotte mainly copied prints in published albums, as when she copied a lithograph to depict one of her characters contemplating the corpse of his mistress. In addition, many of Charlotte's imaginary heroes were patrons of the arts, reflecting her belief that the arts put us in touch with truth and beauty.

Charlotte's writings displayed her vivid imagination. For example, at the age of thirteen she wrote a letter for a fictitious young people's magazine that began, "SIR,—It is well known that Genii have declared that unless they perform certain arduous duties every year, of a mysterious nature, all the world in the firmament will be burnt . . ." The letter went on to describe various powers that the genies claimed to possess, such as the capacity to "reduce the world to a desert" and turn the "purest waters to streams of livid poison." Charlotte concluded by saying that "the horrible wickedness of this needs no remark" and therefore signed off.

In her biography, Gaskell expressed a concern that Charlotte's fantasies were becoming so powerful she was in danger of losing touch with reality. It was therefore good, Gaskell suggested, that Charlotte had so much housework and practical responsibilities; they kept her grounded, balancing fantasy with common sense.

Roe Head

When Charlotte was fourteen, Mr. Brontë sent her to a small boarding school for girls in Roe Head, England. A classmate recalled her impression on the day Charlotte arrived: Charlotte was small and dressed in old-fashioned clothes. She had a strong Irish accent and was "so short-sighted" that she had difficultly seeing what was in front of her. She looked like a "little old woman." She was very shy, nervous, and miserable.

Another classmate remembered how Charlotte stood in the classroom on that first day. She looked out the window at the snowy landscape and cried while the rest of the girls were out at play. Charlotte, the classmate said, was so "sick for home she stood in tears."

Charlotte attended the school at Roe Head for one and a half years. It was a very small school; there were only ten other girls.

Despite Charlotte's initial sadness, her time at Roe Head turned out to be happy. The girls liked her. Charlotte was too frail to participate in their sports, but she had engaging qualities. She could explain paintings in extremely interesting ways. Charlotte also revealed an enthusiasm for political drama that stimulated lively debates. Most of all, Charlotte was an amazing storyteller. The girls loved to lie in their beds at night and listen to her spin tales. Sometimes she made up scary stories—so scary that they could lead to screams of fear.

An Inner Light

Charlotte was sometimes described as plain and odd-looking, and she held this view of herself. Harman says, "The sense of not being attractive haunted Charlotte all her life." But her appearance could also be radiant.

Specifically, there was something about her eyes. According to Gaskell,

> [Her] usual expression was of quiet, listening intelligence; but now and then, on some just occasion for vivid interest or wholesome indignation, a light would shine out, as if some spiritual lamp had been kindled, which glowed behind those expressive orbs.

Gaskell said that when Charlotte's eyes shone, you were hardly aware of anything else about her appearance.

Gaskell, who was Brontë's good friend, knew her only when they were adults. But Gaskell decided to tell readers about this radiant expression in her chapter on Charlotte at Roe Head, apparently guessing that this expression was visible at this time. Because Charlotte's passionate interests and creative imagination found life at Roe Head, the light in her eyes probably did shine brightly when she was there.

It also is likely that this glowing expression emerged earlier, perhaps when she engaged in elaborate imaginary play with her siblings. The children's exciting fantasies lit up their otherwise gloomy lives. As Brontë later wrote in an autobiographical poem, "We created a web in childhood/A web of sunny air." It's easy to imagine how their eyes would have sparkled as they played.

Back Home from Roe Head

At Roe Head, Charlotte formed two strong friendships, with Ellen Nussey and Mary Taylor. These lasted a lifetime. But Charlotte didn't stay at the school. At the age of sixteen, she returned home in order to teach Emily and Anne what she had learned.

All the children were happy to be together again. They resumed their imaginary collaborations and took long walks together on the moors, where, as Charlotte's friend Ellen observed, "Every moss, every flower, every tint and form, were noted and enjoyed."

The children also loved animals. Gaskell reproduced a poem Charlotte wrote about a deer when she was about sixteen. The poem is seven stanzas; here are the first and third:

> Passing the deepest shade
>> Of the wood's somber heart,
> Last night I saw a wounded deer,
>> Laid lonely and apart.
> Pain trembled in his weary limbs,
>> Pain filled his patient eye,
> Pain-crushed amid the shadowy fern
>> His branchy crown did lie.

Teaching at Roe Head

At nineteen Brontë was invited back to Roe Head as a teacher. She didn't want to go, but the family's finances required it.

Brontë's sister Emily went with her to the school as a pupil. But Emily soon became ill. "Nobody knew what ailed her but me," Brontë wrote to Ellen. "I knew only too well." Emily missed home and the moors—a landscape she loved even more deeply than her siblings did. Brontë added that Emily was so depressed that, "I felt in my heart that she would die." So she arranged for Emily to return home, where she recovered.

Brontë hated teaching at the school. She wrote in her personal journal that the students were apathetic, "fat-headed oafs." "Must I from day to day sit chained to this chair prisoned within the four walls, while these glorious summer suns are burning?" She tried to maintain a professional demeanor but fell prey to angry outbursts at her students. Once she even lost her temper with the school's head, Miss Wooler.

As the pressure of teaching mounted, Brontë increasingly drifted into daydreams about Angria. Sometimes she became so lost in her fantasies that she had to be awakened by a school administrator or a student—something she found very annoying. Biographer Harman suggests that this was a time when there was a real risk of a flight into madness.

Some of Brontë's fantasies were erotic, and she felt intense guilt over them. She wrote to Ellen, "If you knew my thoughts; the dreams that absorb me; and the fiery imagination that at times eats me up . . . you would despise me."

Back at home during Christmas breaks, Brontë felt temporarily comfortable. During one break, she and Branwell discussed the vocation they truly wanted to pursue—becoming published authors. They decided to solicit the opinions of established authors.

Branwell wrote to William Wordsworth and received no reply. Charlotte wrote to the England's poet laureate, Robert Southey, asking if he thought she had the talent to pursue a literary career. She sent him a poem, along with an account of one of her daydream visions.

Southey wrote back with a warning that her daydreams could "induce a distempered state of mind." He said Brontë should give up her literary ambitions and concentrate on the duties fitted for women. She replied that she was already fully engaged in her responsibilities as a teacher of children, but she would take his advice and give up her wish to become a writer. Of course, she didn't.

Miss Wooler exercised great patience with Brontë. Miss Wooler even forgave her angry outbursts. But when the school moved to a new location, the rooms were damp and weakened Brontë's health. The dampness also produced upsetting thoughts of Cowan Bridge. Gaskell reported that Brontë's condition worsened and she "would turn sick and trembling at any sudden noise, and could hardly repress her screams when startled." Miss Wooler called in a doctor, who insisted that Brontë return home. There, the doctor said, the company of those she loved and the weather could save her life and her sanity. She did return home, and after a week of bed rest, she recovered.

Governess

As Brontë neared the age of twenty-one, life held few hopes. Most young women were eager to marry, but she was not. The institution seemed dreary and stifling. As Harman says, "Spiritual communion, yes; love, sex, the sublime, yes;" but not "the conventional female fate of marriage and motherhood." But her vocational prospects were limited. Other than teaching, the principal opportunity was that of governess. She tried it several times.

Brontë's views on the governess role are found in letters to Emily and friends. "I used to think I should like to be in the stir of grand folks' society," Brontë said, "but I have had enough of it." She felt the position rendered her invisible. "[My employer] does not know my character & she does not wish to know it." All her employer cared about was "the greatest quantity of labor" that could be "squeezed out of me." While her employer and friends held conversations, Brontë felt like she was forced "to look on and listen to fools" and then "wipe their children's noses, fetch and carry things or sit hemming their sheets."

Brontë yearned for something more. As she wrote to Ellen, she felt an inner urge to break out of her social circumstances and fulfill "faculties unexercised."

Farewell to Angria

At the age of twenty-three, Brontë decided to abandon her Angrian fantasies and take a new look at what the real world might offer. She had no luck. She and her sisters attempted to create their own school, but no pupils applied. She went to Brussels to learn French and fell in love with her married teacher, but he didn't reciprocate. As the years wore on, Brontë increasingly stayed home in Haworth to care for her father, who was losing his eyesight. At twenty-nine, she wrote, "One day resembles another . . . life wears away. I shall soon be thirty; and I have done nothing yet. I feel as if we were all buried here."

A Magnificent Discovery

Then things changed. One day she stumbled across poetry secretly written by Emily. The poems, Brontë said, "stirred my heart like the sound of a trumpet." They were "not common effusions, not at all like the poetry women generally write." The poems were "terse, vigorous, and genuine. To my ear, they had also a peculiar music— wild, melancholy, and elevating. . . . No woman that ever lived—ever wrote such poetry before."

Emily's poems dealt with loss and despair. She even wrote about the feelings of a young woman in prison. A poem that undoubtedly resonated with Brontë was titled "To Imagination." It concluded,

> I trust not thy phantom bliss,
>
> Yet, still, in evening's quiet hour,
>
> With never-failing thankfulness,
>
> I welcome thee, Benignant Power;
>
> Sure solacer of human cares,
>
> And sweeter hope, when hope despairs!

Initially, Emily was angry at Charlotte for reading poems that she had kept secret. Then Anne came forward with poems of her own, and Emily finally agreed to try to publish a collection of poems by the three of them.

They couldn't get a publisher to print their book at the publisher's expense, so they paid for the project themselves. Using pseudonyms, they titled their book *Poems by Currer, Ellis and Acton Bell*, (preserving their initials, CB, EB, and AB). They used masculine pseudonyms to avoid the criticism that their works were not properly feminine.

They needn't have worried; hardly anyone purchased their book. But before they knew this outcome, they began writing novels, and this time they were determined to get a major publisher to print and promote their works. Charlotte's novel *The Professor* was repeatedly rejected, but by late 1847 when she was thirty-one, the three sisters each had novels in print: Anne's *Agnes Grey*, Emily's *Wuthering Heights*, and Charlotte's *Jane Eyre*. Once again, the sisters wrote under the Bell pseudonyms. *Jane Eyre*, which was largely autobiographical, was the only book to enjoy immediate popularity, but all three eventually became classics.

Although Brontë had given up writing about her imaginary land of Angria several years earlier, some of her earlier fantasy material appeared in the book of poems and her novels. In a scholarly study published in 1941, Fannie Elizabeth Ratchford said that Brontë simply transported many in her cast of Angrians from Africa "to the cooler clime of England." She only changed the characters' names.

Losses and Loneliness

Brontë didn't get much time to enjoy *Jane Eyre*'s success. A year after the book's publication, her three siblings died—and all within a span of eight months. The first funeral was for Branwell, who had been plagued by drug and alcohol addiction. The deaths of Emily and Anne followed. All three succumbed to respiratory illnesses.

Two weeks after her last sister's death, Brontë was resting at the seashore and wrote to her editor about her emotional condition. She confided that she was surprised to be able to manage the losses. "One by one I have watched them fall asleep on my arm—and closed their glazed eyes—and—thus far—God has upheld me. From my heart I thank Him."

But back at Haworth, agony set in. Brontë wrote to Ellen that "Solitude, Remembrance, and Longing" were her sole companions. She believed she could go on with life, but "to sit in a lonely room" with the memory of her losses was a trial she wished no one had to endure.

As *Jane Eyre* took hold of the English literary scene, many people wondered who Currer Bell and the other Bells really were. Two years after the book's publication, a man who had lived in Haworth made the discovery. While reading a more recent Currer Bell novel, *Shirley*, he recognized that some characters spoke in Haworth's local dialectic. The man then guessed that Currer Bell was Charlotte. Soon all three sisters' true identities became known.

Brontë was invited into London's literary society, where she was proud to meet the famous writer William Makepeace Thackeray, who admired her work. However, she was too shy to adjust to the social whirl. The gatherings were exhausting.

After three weeks in London, she returned to Haworth and resumed caring for her father. Her loneliness became awful. As she wrote a friend, there were days and nights "when I felt such a craving for support and companionship as I cannot express. Sleepless, I lay awake night after night, weak and unable to occupy myself."

Some relief came from friends' letters and their occasional visits and, when she felt strong enough, walks along the moors and the countryside. Nature's beauty continued to stir and comfort her.

In addition, Brontë found relief in the creative act of writing. In one letter she confessed to a friend that the last volume of her novel *Shirley* "was composed in the eager, restless endeavor to combat mental sufferings that were scarcely tolerable." "The faculty of imagination lifted me when I was sinking."

Although Brontë was shy, she possessed a genuineness that appealed to people. A local shopkeeper recalled how "Charlotte sometimes would sit and inquire about our circumstances so kindly and feelingly! ... Though I never had any school education, I never felt want of it in her company."

She attracted suitors and turned down three marriage proposals. She finally married a minister named Arthur Bell Nicholls. Brontë enjoyed her marriage very much. She had finally found contentment. But six months after her wedding, she developed an illness associated with pregnancy that caused constant pain. Brontë died three months later, three weeks before her thirty-ninth birthday.

Challenging Conventions

We have seen how Brontë's imagination sometimes worried her biographers; they believed it threatened her sanity. We also have seen how her imagination helped her get through suffering and produce great writing.

Brontë's imagination also enlarged her vision of her social world. It enabled her to think beyond the conventions that others accepted as givens. She especially sought new possibilities for women. She railed against the role of the governess, daring to imagine "faculties unexercised." She also embraced Emily's poetry because it was wild and ventured beyond conventional feminine writing. As she said, "No woman that ever lived—ever wrote such poetry before." And she herself pursued a literary career that violated the social norms that Poet Laureate Southey and society in general imposed on women.

Brontë wrote about the condition of women in many of her letters. In one, she observed that restrictions on women begin early in the socialization process: "Girls are protected as if they were something very frail or silly indeed, while boys are turned loose on the world as if they—of all beings in existence, were the wisest and least liable to be led astray."

In Brontë's time, and to some extent in our time as well, women feared growing into an "old maid." Brontë looked at this lifestyle in a new way:

> I speculate much on the existence of unmarried and never-to-be married women now-a-days; and I have already got to the point of considering that there is no more respectable character on this earth than the unmarried woman, who makes her own way through life quietly, perseveringly, without the support of husband or brother.

Jane Eyre

Brontë forcefully defied conventions in her novel *Jane Eyre*. For one thing, she broke with tradition by refusing to make Jane, her heroine, beautiful. It is reported that her sisters told her a heroine must be beautiful to be interesting, to which Brontë replied: "I will prove you wrong; I will show you a heroine as plain and as small as myself, who shall be as interesting as any of yours."

The novel begins with Jane as a ten-year-old and is narrated by Jane herself. According to Harman, *Jane Eyre* was the very first novel to use a first-person child narrator.

Departing from her own life story, Brontë made Jane an orphan who is cruelly mistreated by her aunt. Jane also speaks her mind to an extent Brontë undoubtedly did not.

Jane hopes to be sent away to school, and she is interviewed by a minister who has the authority to accept her or not. He asks her about the Bible, and instead of telling him what he wants to hear, Jane tells the truth:

> "And the Psalms?" he asks. "I hope you like them?"
> "No sir." . . . "Psalms are not interesting."

Jane's aunt takes Jane's "insolence" as an opportunity to criticize the child. She tells the minister that she has "tendency to deceit," and if he decides to accept her, the staff will need to keep a close eye on her.

Jane says nothing and stifles a sob. After the minister departs, the aunt orders Jane to her room. But Jane hesitates. She wants to speak up for herself:

> *Speak* I must: I had been trodden on severely, and *must* turn but how? . . . I gathered my energies and launched them into this blunt sentence:— "I am not deceitful: if I were, I should say I loved *you*; but I declare I do not love you . . ."

> Ere I had finished this reply, my soul began to expand, to exult, with the strangest sense of freedom, of triumph, I ever felt. It seemed as if an invisible bond had burst, and that I had struggled out into unhoped-for liberty.

Harman says "the first readers of *Jane Eyre* were, understandably, bowled over . . ." Everyone knew about children's anger, but no one had dared to write about it this way—to express the sense of freedom Jane's rebellion released. Jane's first-person accounts, Harman says, "were like dispatches from a new frontier."

Later Jane becomes a governess. Jane is treated much better by her employer than Brontë was, but the job's confinement gnaws at Jane, too. She wants to pursue farther-reaching possibilities. She says that her sole relief is to walk along the upper hallway of the house and let her "mind's eye dwell on whatever bright visions" that arise . . . Brontë doesn't spell out the nature of Jane's visions, but hints that they are similar to Brontë's own fantasies as a young adult.

Jane then says that millions of people share her feeling of confinement in their social roles.

> Nobody knows how many rebellions besides political rebellions ferment in the masses of life which people earth. Women are supposed to be very calm generally; but women feel just as men feel; they need exercise for their faculties, and a field for their efforts as much as their brothers do; they suffer from too rigid a constraint.

Jane adds that "it is narrow-minded in their more privileged fellow-creatures to say that they ought to confine themselves to making puddings and knitting stockings." For women seek to do more than custom allows.

Conclusion

Brontë was a woman of exceptional imagination. Her fantasies were sometimes so vivid that at one point, when teaching at Roe Head, they affected her mental stability. But the fantasies kept her going. They provided relief from drudgery and the pain of enormous loss. What's more, her imagination fueled stunning literary works and yearnings for a freer life—a life outside the bounds of rigid customs.

And her imagination had its origins in her childhood play with her siblings. As Brontë wrote in the beginning lines of her most widely cited poem,

> We wove a web in childhood,
>
> A web of sunny air

The "web of sunny air" was too powerful to fade. Throughout her life, despite all her losses and bleak times, the light of her childhood imagination continued to shine.

~ 4 ~

Howard Thurman

· · · · · · ·

A Minister Builds on His Childhood Sense of the Unity of Life

We are all tied together.

—Howard Thurman

In 1935, Howard Thurman, a young professor of religion at Howard University, and three other African American leaders visited Ceylon, Burma, and India. In India, Thurman met with Mohandas Gandhi, who was engaged in the struggle to free India from British rule. When Thurman returned to the United States, he gave lectures on Gandhi's method of nonviolent resistance. Thurman's lectures introduced Gandhi to the U.S. civil rights movement.

Thurman's visit to Asia also stimulated his own thinking. The trip was sponsored by the YMCA and YWCA, and during the tour Thurman was asked tough questions about Christianity. How could Thurman, a Black man, represent Christianity when most of the slave traders and Americans who oppressed his people were Christians?

And if Christianity had real power to improve society, why hadn't it eradicated racism? Gandhi himself pointed to these problems when he and Thurman met.

Thurman believed the questions were good ones. Christianity, as an institutional movement, had often sided with the powerful over the oppressed. But Thurman also believed that the teachings of Jesus offer profound hope, and he began articulating a religious vision that honors freedom, equality, and universal love. At their deepest level, Thurman's views were rooted in his mystical experiences of the unity of all life—experiences that began when he was a child playing in nature.

Beginnings

Howard Thurman (1899–1981) grew up in Daytona, Florida. He was the youngest of three children, with two older sisters. His father, who laid track for a railroad, died when Howard was seven years old. His mother was an emotionally distant woman who worked long hours cooking for white people. The children were primarily raised by their maternal grandmother Nancy Ambrose, a former slave and a midwife. She also contributed to the family's finances by doing laundry for white people.

Daytona was quite segregated. Young Howard attended an all-Black elementary school and had to be careful not to be spotted in white areas after dark.

Prejudice often appeared in unexpected ways. Thurman remembered a day when he was raking leaves for a white family. Their daughter teased him by messing up the piles he created, and when Howard asked her to stop, she jabbed him in the hand with a pin. When he drew back in pain, she said, "Oh, Howard, that didn't hurt you! You can't feel!'

Howard's grandmother was very sensitive to racism's effects on the children's self-esteem. When she sensed that the children's self-confidence was flagging, she told them about a Black preacher who had come to her plantation once or twice a year to preach to the slaves. She gave the sermons just as she remembered them. At the end of each, the preacher had paused, scrutinized every face, and proclaimed: "You are not slaves! You are God's children!" When the grandmother said these words to the children, she would stiffen her spine, and when she finished talking, the children's spirits were restored.

Nature

Despite their grandmother's care, Howard was often lonely, and he found comfort in nature. For example, the night provided a kind of maternal reassurance. "The night," he later wrote "seemed to cover my spirit like a gentle blanket." At times when the night was still,

> I could hear the night think, and feel the night feel. This comforted me and I found myself wishing the night would hurry and come. I felt embraced, enveloped, held secure . . .

Howard told the night his most private thoughts. "When things went badly during the day, I would sort them out in the dark as I lay in my bed, cradled by the night sky."

The woods, too, befriended him, as did an old oak tree that had withstood many storms.

> I needed the strength of that tree, and, like it, I wanted to hold my ground. Eventually, I discovered

that the oak tree and I had a unique relationship. I could sit, my back against its trunk, and feel the same peace that would come to me in my bed at night.

Leaning against the tree, Howard found that, "I could reach down in the quiet places of my spirit, take out my bruises and my joys, unfold them, and talk about them. I could talk aloud to the oak tree and know that I was understood."

His most intense experiences came at the seashore. When he walked along the shore at night, and the sea was still,

> I had the sense that all things, the sand, the sea, the stars, the night, and I were one lung through which all life breathed. Not only was I aware of a vast rhythm enveloping all, but I was part of it and it was part of me.

Even the storms seemed to embrace young Howard, and his experiences of unity with nature gave him "a certain overriding immunity against much of the pain with which I would have to deal in the years ahead when the ocean was only a memory. The sense held: I felt rooted in life, in nature, in existence."

Schooling

Howard performed exceptionally well in school, but the school for Black children in Daytona only went up to the seventh grade. The school's principal tutored him for an additional year, and he was set to attend a high school in Jacksonville, where a cousin offered to provide him with room and board in exchange for chores.

Howard said good-bye to his family and friends, went to the train station, and purchased a ticket. But the agent told him he needed to pay for his trunk as well. He didn't have the money, and he sat down and cried. Then he looked up and saw a Black man in work shoes, overalls, and a denim cap. The man asked, "Boy, what in hell are you crying about?" When Howard told him, the man said, "If you're trying to get out of this damn town to get an education, the least I can do is help you." The stranger paid for his trunk and walked away.

Thurman never saw the man again, but he dedicated his autobiography, *With Head and Heart*, "To the stranger in the railroad station in Daytona Beach who restored my broken dream sixty-five years ago."

After high school, Thurman attended Morehouse College, a historically Black college for men in Atlanta. He won several literary prizes and was the class valedictorian. But of all the events at Morehouse, Thurman highlighted the manner in which the college's president, John Hope, addressed the students. Hope always called the students "young gentlemen." White people, Thurman said, never referred to any African American man with such respect. They always called him "boy" or worse. "No wonder," Thurman said, "that every time Dr. Hope addressed us as 'young gentlemen,' the seeds of self-worth and confidence, long dormant, began to germinate and sprout."

By his senior year in college, Thurman was certain he wanted to become a minister. In his autobiography, he said he had never been clear about the reasons for this choice. He had simply felt that religion was his calling.

Developing a Philosophy

After college Thurman studied at the Rochester Theological Seminary, where he was one of only two African American students in his class. Initially, he felt socially isolated, but he was excited to roam through the library's vast stacks and read widely. And he soon became friends with other students. In fact, he was elected president of the student government.

While at the seminary, Thurman attended a retreat in upstate New York and was introduced to the writings of Olive Schreiner. Schreiner, who had died a few years earlier, was a white South African feminist and opponent of colonialism. Some of Schreiner's writings were dreamlike adventures which, Thurman said, took him into "a wonderland of the spirit and imagination." Thurman emphasized that Schreiner possessed "an instinctual sense of the unity of all life," and her writings confirmed the value of his boyhood nature experiences in which he felt part of everything around him.

Thurman observed that he might have felt uneasy about the fact that Schreiner was a white woman, but he did not. Their shared belief in the unity of life was too strong. It overcame their differences in ethnicity, nationality, and culture.

Thurman earned his divinity degree in 1926, at the age of twenty-six. That year, he married Kate Kelley, a young social worker, and became the pastor of the Mount Zion Baptist Church in Oberlin, Ohio. The couple named their first child Olive, after Olive Schreiner.

In his second year at Oberlin, Thurman chanced upon a second-hand book sale that offered any book for ten cents. He purchased a small volume by Rufus Jones, a professor at Haverford College in Pennsylvania. Jones was a Quaker pacifist who identified himself as a mystic. Thurman was so stimulated by Jones's ideas that he left his position in Oberlin to spend six months as a fellow at Haverford under Jones's mentorship.

Studying with Jones, Thurman learned that his childhood experiences of the unity of life fit into religion's mystical tradition. He had experienced the kinds of immediate, personal insights that mystics value. Thurman also learned that mystics haven't all retreated into their own, private worlds. They have engaged in social action. This fact was important to Thurman because he wanted to promote racial equality.

Schreiner and Jones, then, helped Thurman begin forming a philosophy based on the mystical insight into the unity of life. That is, he began to feel that because people are basically one, part of all life, social harmony and equality are possible.

Tragedy and Ocean Voyages

Thurman next accepted a joint appointment at Morehouse and Spelman Colleges, the latter a historically Black college for women in Atlanta. He taught courses in religion and philosophy. But Thurman had only been at the colleges for three semesters when his wife Kate died of tuberculosis. Shaken and exhausted, he sought restoration in an ocean voyage to Europe.

Crossing the Atlantic Ocean for the first time, he had experiences similar to those of his childhood. As he later wrote, "There were times when standing alone on the deck, the boundaries of self dimmed and almost disappeared." Thurman said the voyage "was like a homecoming of the spirit." When he returned to the United States, he felt renewed and ready to move forward.

In 1932, he married Sue Bailey, a historian and activist, and accepted a faculty position at Howard University in Washington, DC. Soon he began thinking about a trip to Burma, Ceylon, and India and a meeting with Gandhi. Although he wanted to go, he had reservations. He correctly anticipated that he would be seen as an apologist for American Christians who supported segregation. So when he decided to make the voyage, it was with a degree of trepidation.

Once again, the ocean gave him strength. There were days and nights when the sea raged and flung the ship about. Thurman loved the sensations, feeling the raw energy of the water at the roots of his being. When the sea calmed and the morning sun shone, he and Sue looked at the horizon and felt at one with the "whole sweep of the world." Everything seemed "undifferentiated in a moment of time." These experiences reprised Thurman's childhood feelings of being part of something vast and powerful, and the experiences undoubtedly gave him confidence for dealing with the challenges ahead.

When Thurman's Asian hosts criticized his religion for supporting racism, he didn't react defensively. He listened openly and actually agreed. But he nevertheless felt that Jesus's message of love could free his people and uplift everyone. So he began to formulate his interpretation of Jesus's teaching.

A Message of Love

Thurman published his fullest statement on this topic in a book titled *Jesus and the Disinherited*. He began by pointing to parallels in the social circumstances of Jesus and African Americans. Both were completely vulnerable to aggressive state forces. Both lacked rights. "If a

Roman soldier pushed Jesus into a ditch, he could not appeal to Caesar; he would be just another Jew in the ditch." The situation, Thurman said, is similar for African Americans—indeed for "all the cast-down people of every generation and in every age."

Thurman described how the oppressed fear and hate their oppressors. Many feel they must be prepared, at a moment's notice, to protect their lives. Some turn to weapons and violence for self-defense.

Thurman recognized hatred's appeal. Society may judge one as insignificant, but hatred gives one a sense of strength. One rises up in righteous indignation. The individual says, "I will not bow; I will fight," and he or she gains self-respect.

But Thurman observed that hatred soon gets out of control. Consumed by hate, the individual is ready to lash out at everyone. There is no effort to understand the circumstances others might be under. The hater tears everyone down. Ethical values based on respect for others disintegrate.

What's more, Thurman said, hate dries up the springs of creativity. Negativity leaves no room for the nurturing of positive ideas. Thurman summed up his position by saying, "Hatred is destructive to hated and hater alike."

Following Jesus, Thurman wanted people to replace hate with love—even for their enemies. He recognized that this is far from easy but pointed out that people do not need to love their enemies' *actions* or their *way of life*. They only need to love them as *fellow humans*. To love the Roman tax collector, Jesus had to see him not in his government role but as a human being. Similarly, the African American must "see the individual white man in the context of a common humanity."

The same obligation applies to the socially privileged: They, too, must find common identity with all people. Thurman quoted the socialist Eugene Debs: "While there is a lower class, I am in it. While there is a criminal element, I am in it. While there is a man in jail, I am not free."

Thurman's belief in people's common humanity was strengthened by his mystical experiences. During mystical states, he said, the individual feels part of something very powerful that is present in all life. The person feels a universal spirit that knows "no age, no race, no culture, and no condition of men." This spirit undergirds the difficult work of overcoming social barriers and appealing to the simple heart that is common to all.

Pastoral Leader

As a person who believed in the unity of all people, Thurman advocated for integration rather than Black separatist movements. In 1943, he gave up his tenured position at Howard University and went to San Francisco to start the first multiracial, intercultural church in the United States.

He encountered numerous difficulties. For example, the first time he went to a hospital to visit a parishioner, the desk nurse wouldn't let him on the ward because he was Black. Only when someone recognized him as the minister the patient had requested was Thurman allowed in. But Thurman never permitted such events to weaken him, and the church was a success.

In addition, Thurman provided spiritual counseling to numerous activists, including Martin Luther King Jr., Jesse Jackson, James Farmer, and Bayard Rustin. Even these brave leaders suffered bouts of discouragement and self-doubt, and talks with Thurman helped them regain their strength. As historians Catherine Tumber and Walter Earl Fluker say, somehow Thurman "was able to dig deep into the inner recesses of one's being, in the places which for others seemed unreachable, and to find the hidden treasures of the soul—the lost dreams wandering about as forsaken ghosts in the wastelands of the heart, the shattered hopes that had ricocheted off the hard realities of living."

Thurman didn't engage in protest marches or civil disobedience. Consequently, he is not nearly as well-known as King, Jackson, Rosa Parks, and many others. But within the civil rights movement, Thurman was recognized as its pastoral leader. King is said to have carried Thurman's *Jesus and the Disinherited* in his briefcase during the peak of the movement.

Meditations of the Heart

We don't know the contents of Thurman's private meetings with the civil rights leaders; these are confidential. But in his book *Meditations of the Heart* Thurman described how meditation and prayer can bring us peace and restore our spirits.

Quiet meditation, Thurman said, is valuable for everyone. There are times when we all need refuge from life's stresses and strains. Overburdened and exhausted, we yearn for "some haven, some place of retreat, some time of quiet where our bruised and shredded spirits may find healing and restoration."

Thurman recommended that we sit silently and engage in introspection. We should examine some part of ourselves, turning it over and viewing it from different angles. In the process, we should ask: What is the end of our doings? What are our highest purposes? When we takes stock in this way, quiet changes begin to take place. At some moment in the stillness we sense a deeper tone. We feel the peace that comes from being rooted in something positive that far transcends ourselves. Our spirits are refreshed.

Thurman believed that the feelings of rootedness gained from meditation give us strength in our daily lives. We no longer feel alone and adrift. We are no longer battered by life's storms and subject to others' approval. We can stand up to society's pressures and prejudices because we are grounded in a much greater presence.

In *Meditations of the Heart*, Thurman identified this presence as God. Others have preferred to refer to it as an all-encompassing spirit, while some have left it undefined. In any case, Thurman maintained that this presence is to be found everywhere because "all life is one." All living things and everything around them are manifestations of a single whole.

Concluding Thoughts

As we have seen, Thurman's mystical belief in the unity of life originated in childhood. His most dramatic early experience occurred when he walked along the beach at night. He said, "I had the sense that all things, the sand, the sea, the stars, the night, and I were one lung through which all life breathed." Thurman's belief in the unity of life nourished his hope for human progress. He felt that we can overcome social divisions and love one another because we are all part of the great community of life.

I would add that Thurman's early nature experiences also informed his approach to meditation and prayer. When he was under the oak tree or the cover of the night, young Thurman sorted out his thoughts, hopes, and injuries—and he continued to engage in the same activities during his later meditations and prayers.

In addition, childhood nature experiences made Thurman sensitive to the way meditation and prayer provide a sense of security and stability. As a child, he felt "embraced" and "held secure" by the night. Leaning against the oak tree, he felt its strength and its ability to withstand storms. At the ocean, he felt "rooted in life, in nature, in existence." So when similar sensations—sensations of being rooted in something larger than himself—emerged in adult meditation, he appreciated them.

∽

Extended Discussion on the Unity of Life

Thurman's writings present us with a puzzle. His belief in the unity of life emerged from his childhood experiences in nature—yet his writing often relegated nature to a secondary role. Instead of discussing the natural environment as a vital part of life, he quickly turned his attention to human life. For example, he said that the mystic's vision includes a sense of "unity with all life, particularly human life."

Why didn't he give more attention to nature?

In one essay Thurman suggested that, ironically, nature is too perfect. If we allow ourselves to become caught up in its beautiful harmonies, we can lose sight of the discord in human affairs. Our urgent task, he said, is to understand that all humans are one and to create harmony within the fractured human family.

But when Thurman was in his seventies and the last decade of his life, his view changed. He saw nature in disarray. Humans, he observed, have inflicted terrible damage on it. We have polluted the air, poisoned the waters, and decimated the forests. We have driven many species to extinction.

Underlying these actions, Thurman said, is our assumption that we are separate from and superior to nature. We fail to realize that we are part of it. We do not appreciate the wisdom of the Native American statement that we are children of the earth. And as a result of our destruction, we do not feel comfortable in nature as our home. Instead, we suffer from feelings of rootlessness. isolation, and anguish.

It is my impression that even in his last writings Thurman's first concern was the unity of human life. But he passionately asserted that all life, whatever form it takes, is one.

☞ 5 ☜

Jane Goodall

· · · · · · ·

Feeling Part of a Unifying Power

I have been privileged to know the peace of the forest.
—Jane Goodall

Jane Goodall is the world's most famous animal researcher. In 1960, at the age of twenty-six, she ventured into an African forest and made important discoveries about the social lives of chimpanzees. In recent decades, however, she has spent little time in the forest. Instead, she has traveled the world to tell people that chimpanzees are threatened with extinction. She also warns audiences about the viability of the planet itself.

Audiences are a bit surprised to discover that Goodall, despite her fame, is an unassuming woman who has held on to aspects of her childhood. She talks lovingly about a stuffed toy chimpanzee she has had since she was one year old, and she carries a stuffed monkey doll to the podium with her. The doll, which she calls Mr. H, was a gift from Gary Haun, a U.S. Marine who lost his eyesight in war but nevertheless became an outstanding magician.

Goodall also frequently says hello to audiences in chimpanzee language—a rising series of hoots. She has no qualms about demonstrating a childhood pleasure in dolls and animal sounds.

And Goodall's childhood attitudes extend much further. In this chapter, I will highlight ways in which her youthful outlook has helped her to understand chimpanzees, formulate a personal philosophy, and get through personal difficulties.

Early Years

Jane Goodall (b. 1934) was born in London and lived much of her childhood in Bournemouth, a seaside resort town on the English Channel. Her father, Mortimer, was an engineer and race car driver. He was handsome and charming but took little interest in his daughter's upbringing. Jane's mother, Vanne, had been a secretary for a show business entrepreneur before her marriage. She then became a full-time homemaker. Jane had one sibling, a younger sister, and for a while, an imaginary companion who could fly. In addition to Vanne, Jane's grandmother, Danny, and a nanny, Nancy Sowden, were loving caregivers.

Jane's family had limited financial means. It had enough money for necessities, but there wasn't enough for "luxuries" such as a bicycle. The family members attended the local Congregational church.

Jane was always fascinated by animals. At eighteen months of age, she took a handful of earthworms to bed with her. "Jane," her mother said, "if you keep them here, they'll die. They need the earth." So Jane hurriedly took the worms back to the garden.

When Jane was four, she visited her grandmother's farm and was determined to see how chickens lay eggs. First, she followed a chicken into the henhouse, but the chicken squawked and ran away. So she tried another approach. She went into the henhouse before the hen arrived and silently waited for the hen to enter and lay an egg. Finally, she saw how the hen did it and rushed back to the house. Jane had been gone for nearly four hours—so long the family had called the police to try to find her. Her mother must have been angry, but Goodall says, "She did not scold me. She noticed my shining eyes and sat down to listen to the story of how a hen lays an egg." Her mother decided that the important thing was her child's sense of wonder.

Young Jane's life wasn't always pleasant. When she was five and a half, England declared war on Germany, and the war was constantly on everyone's mind. When Jane was twelve, her parents divorced.

Jane wasn't keen on school, either. But her interest in nature continued, and she found comfort in it. She spent hours in the family's garden, and she especially loved a tree she called Beech, with which she felt a strong connection:

> There, high above the ground, I could feel a part
> of the life of the tree, swaying when the wind blew
> strongly, close to the rustling of the leaves. The songs
> of the birds sounded different up there—clearer and
> louder. I could sometimes lay my cheek against
> the trunk and seem to feel the sap, the lifeblood of
> Beech, coursing through the rough bark.

The tree gave Jane a place to be by herself and think. She thought about the horrors of the war, the Holocaust, and the dropping of the atomic bombs. These events affected her deeply and made her question her belief in a benevolent God.

From the age of eight or nine, Jane dreamed of living among animals in Africa. Her favorite books were the Doctor Dolittle series, about a man who learned to talk to animals and traveled to Africa to help monkeys who were dying from a horrible illness. She soon turned to the Tarzan books, about the English boy raised by apes. In warm weather she read her books in the top branches of Beech. As she told Dale Peterson, her biographer, "I think I went through all the Tarzan books thirty feet or so above the ground." She added that she was "madly in love" with Tarzan, and "terribly jealous of Jane." Jane's reading material expanded, but she kept returning to the Doctor Dolittle and Tarzan books, even at the ages of sixteen and seventeen.

At sixteen, Jane also developed a crush on the town's new young minister and took a new interest in religion. Although she didn't think parts of the Bible make logical sense, she found meaning and poetic beauty in it.

At this age, Jane wrote poetry herself, some of which spoke of a spiritual presence in nature. For example, she concluded a poem about a duck with these lines:

The lovely dunes; the setting sun;
The duck—and I;
One spirit, moving timelessly
Beneath the sky.

Looking back on this poem years later, Goodall says she was beginning to feel part of some kind of "great unifying power," which she identified as God.

After high school, Goodall wanted to attend a university but lacked the funds. Her mother told her that a secretary could get a job anywhere in the world, so with the hope of one day traveling to Africa, she went to London for secretarial training. She continued to read widely and enrolled in some free evening classes in literature, journalism, and spirituality.

Africa

While working as a secretary, she received an unexpected letter from a childhood friend who had moved to Kenya. The friend asked if she would like to visit. It was a thrilling moment. To save money for the trip, Goodall gave up an apartment rental in London, moved back with her family, and worked hard as a waitress.

The ocean voyage to Africa was fun, but Goodall was most impressed by the ocean itself. Like Howard Thurman, she had a feeling of oneness with it. She felt she was part of the "limitless world of water and air, sun and stars and wind." This feeling strengthened her belief in a spiritual power that surrounds and includes us.

A few weeks after arriving in Kenya, Goodall was riding home from a dinner party when someone told her that if she was interested in animals, she should talk to Louis Leakey. Leakey was the curator of Nairobi's natural history museum. With the talents of a showman, Leakey had gained wide recognition for the various fossils and primitive tools he had unearthed in collaboration with his wife Mary. Leakey was impressed by Goodall's enthusiasm and knowledge of animals, and he hired her as his personal secretary.

Goodall liked working in the museum. She learned a great deal about animals and African tribes. But she couldn't accept the killing that had taken place to collect so many specimens of the same species. She felt it was a "slaughter of the innocents."

Each year, Louis and Mary Leakey spent three months digging for fossils in Tanzania's Olduvai Gorge on the Serengeti plains. They had found primitive stone tools but not the remains of our early ancestors who made them. In her first year on the job, Goodall joined the Leakeys on their annual dig. It was hard work, but she found it fascinating. There were times when she was filled with awe by the fossilized bone she held in her hand—a bone that had "once been part of a living, breathing animal" who had lived in primeval times.

This was in 1957. Two years later, the Leakeys unearthed one of the oldest humanlike fossils that scientists had seen.

In an autobiographical book for young people, *My Life with the Chimpanzees*, Goodall said she could have gone on working at the museum, or she could have pursued a career as a paleontologist, searching for fossils. But these careers meant working with dead animals. She wanted to fulfill her childhood dream of being among living animals. "Somehow," she wrote,

> I must find a way to watch free, wild animals living their own, undisturbed lives. I wanted to learn things that no one else knew, uncover secrets through patient observation. I wanted to come as close to talking to animals as I could, to be like Doctor Dolittle. I wanted to move among them without fear, like Tarzan.

When Jane was with Leakey at the Olduvai Gorge, he told her that he wished someone would study chimpanzees in the wild—a study that no one had yet attempted for any length of time. He believed that the behavior of chimps, as humans' closest living relatives, would shine light on humans' distant past. He reasoned that any behavior shared by chimpanzees and humans might have been present in a common ancestor who had lived several million years ago.

For several days, Leakey talked to Goodall about the need to study chimpanzees in the wild. When he finally told her that she was the researcher he had in mind, she was quite surprised. After all, she didn't even have a college degree. But Leakey said he wasn't looking for someone whose mind was cluttered with academic concepts. He wanted someone with an open mind, a love of animals, and great patience. Goodall later wrote, "When he put it like that, of course, I had to admit that I was the perfect choice."

After considerable effort, Leakey raised money to support Goodall's field research for four months in the Gombe Stream Reserve in Tanzania. The reserve, which is only about twenty square miles, is on the eastern shore of Lake Tanganyika. It is very hilly, with beautiful forests, and it provides legal protection to the chimpanzees within its boundaries.

First Studies in Gombe

Goodall arrived in Gombe in July 1960. The British government refused to allow a white woman to venture alone in the bush, so Goodall's mother accompanied her.

When the two women arrived, the villagers suspected that they were spies. A resourceful Tanzanian park wildlife official brokered an agreement: Goodall could go into the forest to observe chimpanzees if she hired three villagers to go with her. The villagers would serve as porters and scouts, and in one case, as a monitor to check on her work.

When the monitor found out that Goodall's expeditions involved climbing mountains, he bowed out. So, accompanied by two villagers, Goodall began daily hikes. Her mother remained at the base camp, where she met with visitors, dispensed simple medical supplies such as bandages to the villagers, and worked on a novel.

Goodall had envisioned doing her fieldwork alone, and her aides slowed her down. In addition, she believed that the chimpanzees, who were wary of humans, were even warier when more than one human came in sight. But she carried on.

Goodall found a favorite peak from which she could observe chimpanzees with her binoculars, but several hours often went by before she spotted any, and she couldn't see them in any detail. Sometimes she tried to get closer to them, but they fled.

It must have been tempting to try methods that promised quicker results. For example, other pioneering researchers hid behind blinds where the chimps wouldn't see them, so the chimps wouldn't run away. But Goodall wanted to be open about her presence and gradually win the chimpanzees' trust.

So Goodall exercised great patience. Sometimes she stayed at the peak, and whenever she followed the chimpanzees in the forest, she got only as close as their comfort level allowed. When her movements made them uneasy, she pretended that she had no interest in them. She acted as if she were just another primate, looking for food. She hoped that they would eventually lose their fear of her and conduct their natural behavior in her presence.

After a month, there was a small breakthrough. One of the chimpanzees, a distinguished looking male with a grey beard, demonstrated less fear. He accidentally passed within ten yards of Goodall. Initially he was shocked to see her. He then circled around the area and peered at her with calm curiosity.

Three months later the same chimpanzee, whom Goodall called David Greybeard, sat down only fifteen yards from her and watched her "with absolutely no fear." He simply "rubbed his chin."

But the other chimps continued to fear her, and Goodall was worried. Her four-month project was nearing its end without any discoveries that would justify extended funding. Then she had a helpful visit from George Schaller, who had recently studied gorillas in the Belgian Congo. He had used the same unobtrusive approach as Goodall, and he understood her need for more time. Schaller suggested that if she could see chimps eating meat or using a tool, she probably would obtain further funding.

The discovery of meat-eating would be important because at the time everyone assumed that the chimpanzee diet was entirely vegetarian. And during her third month in Gombe, she did see chimps eating flesh, probably that of an infant bushpig.

More significantly, a few days later she saw David Greybeard and another male, whom she later named Goliath, using twigs as tools. Each chimp stripped a twig of its leaves, poked it into a hole in the ground, pulled it up with termites clutching onto it, and ate them.

It was difficult for Goodall to believe what she had seen. Researchers had previously seen chimps and gorillas engaged in behavior that could be called tool *use*. For example, they used rocks to pound open nuts. But by stripping the twigs of their leaves, the chimps engaged in a simple kind of tool*making*. This was thought to be one of the defining capacities of our species, possessed by humans alone. As Goodall says, her observation "challenged human uniqueness."

Goodall's discoveries of meat-eating and toolmaking led to a National Geographic Society grant that enabled her to continue her fieldwork. And now the authorities allowed Goodall to continue her research alone, without assistants and her mother as a chaperone.

Like a Child in a Magical Forest

When Goodall discovered chimps eating meat and making tools, she was not exploring in an open-minded way. She had predetermined ideas about what she wanted to find. But when she received a new grant, she felt the "pressure was off"; she had time to openly take in the forest that seemed so magical to her. Even when days passed without her sighting chimpanzees, she wasn't disappointed. Instead, she became fascinated by whatever she encountered—insects, birds, baboons and their playful youngsters, the lovely sighing sounds of the lake. Each day presented something new. Goodall says she experienced nature in the manner of a young child, for whom, Goodall says, "everything is fresh and much of it is wonderful."

Goodall tried to experience nature without words and labels. Verbal categories, she says, can be useful, but they also can close off our experience. For example, when we encounter an insect, we label it and go on our way.

We don't take time to fully consider its appearance or behavior, which may be quite remarkable. Goodall likened her wordless experience of the forest to that of a young child, whose sensations are not yet dominated by verbal categories.

As she spent time alone in the forest, she increasingly felt oneness with it. As when she was a child, she "became intensely aware of the being-ness of trees." Feeling the bark of "an ancient forest giant, or the cool skin of a young and eager sapling, gave me a strange, intuitive sense of the sap as it was sucked up by unseen roots and drawn up to the very tips of the branches, high overhead."

Goodall's sense of oneness with the forest included a sense of its peacefulness, which "reached into the inner core of my being." Goodall says that she is often asked: Given all the turmoil in the world, how do you remain so peaceful? Her answer is that she carries the peace of the forest within her.

Feeling continuity with the forest, Goodall engaged in childlike talk with it. That is, she talked out loud to things as if they were friends who could understand her: "'Good morning, Peak,' I would say as I arrived there each morning; 'Hello, Stream,' when I collected my water; 'Oh, Wind, for Heaven's sake, calm down' as it howled overhead."

Goodall's general sense of continuity with nature led to an important set of new observations. Prepared to see chimpanzees as similar to humans, she gave them names and found that chimps, like us, have unique personalities. David Greybeard was calm and gentle. His close friend Goliath was athletic, aggressive, and brave. Flo was a frail-looking older chimp whose appearance was deceiving; she was "tough as nails," and for some reason which mystified human observers, she was very attractive to males. Other chimpanzees were especially clever, mischievous, shy, nurturing, or clownish. And they weren't one-dimensional; they all possessed their own mixture of traits.

Moreover, the chimpanzees revealed the capacity to reflect and plan, and they displayed a wide range of emotions that are common to humans. These emotions included joy, depression, aggression, love, grief, curiosity, and awe.

Even chimpanzees' physical behavior, Goodall discovered, is frequently similar to ours. They, too, kiss, hold hands, embrace, swagger, pirouette, kick, throw, and pat one another on the back. In Goodall's research, differences between humans and chimpanzees steadily dissolved.

Cambridge University

Leakey initially valued Goodall's lack of academic background. But following her discoveries of meat-eating and toolmaking, he decided she needed a degree to give her findings the recognition they deserved. After some effort, he convinced Cambridge University to admit her to its PhD program in ethology. Goodall didn't even have an undergraduate degree, but Cambridge provided her with an expedited program of study, allowing her to spend half her time in Cambridge and half in Gombe. She was eager to attend.

Ethology, the field she would study, was developed by scientists such as Konrad Lorenz and Niko Tinbergen. It was the right field for Goodall; ethologists value the methodological approach that Goodall had taken. Ethologists, that is, believe we should study animals in their natural environment, not in captivity. They also value patient observation as the first step in field research.

But many ethologists, including those at Cambridge at the time, have tried to study animals in a detached, impersonal manner. When Goodall entered Cambridge, in 1962, the ethologists frowned on the way she had given the chimps names (instead of numbers) and how she had described the chimps' personalities, minds, and emotions. They believed Goodall was wrong to treat the chimps as if they were almost human. But Goodall has never wavered in her belief that the chimps are, in fact, much like us.

David Greybeard

The most important chimpanzee in Goodall's research was the bold and gentle male she called David Greybeard. As we have seen, he was the first chimp to tolerate her close approach and the first to provide her with her groundbreaking observations of chimpanzee meat-eating and toolmaking.

Several months after these observations, David Greybeard became the first to visit Goodall's base camp. He entered the site to eat the fruit from an oil-nut palm tree that grew there. On a subsequent visit, he snatched a banana from Goodall's table. Goodall wanted him to feel welcome, so she had a staff member leave bananas for him. After several weeks David Greybeard's friend Goliath accompanied him to the camp. Then others, including Flo and two of her children, visited the camp in search of bananas.

On one occasion, when David came alone, Goodall held a banana out in her hand. He gave a mildly threatening gesture, swaggered from foot to foot, and slapped a nearby tree. Then he gently took the banana out of her hand. Goodall was stirred by this moment of close contact.

The chimps' visits to the camp helped Goodall's research. While in the camp, the chimps were in close proximity to her, enabling her to study behaviors such as childcare and infant development. But the campsite was not the chimps' natural environment. She wasn't studying them in the wild. So she also continued to spend some of her time following them in the forest.

One day David Greybeard came into the camp and then left, vanishing into the thick vegetation. Goodall followed after him. She found him sitting, seemingly waiting. They sat side by side, eating leaves, when she noticed a ripe palm nut on the ground. She offered it to him in the palm of her hand. He took it and dropped it, obviously rejecting her offer, but he gently grasped her hand. Goodall writes,

> I needed no words to understand his message of reassurance: he didn't want the nut, but he understood my motivation, he knew I meant well. To this day I remember the soft pressure of his fingers. We had communicated in a language far more ancient than words.

This communication deepened Goodall's sense of belonging to the natural world. It made her think that she was part of one totality. Goodall has called this event "the most significant of my life."

Cultural Traditions

Goodall's research inspired other scientists to study chimpanzees in different African sites. Goodall was impressed by several differences in chimpanzee behavior, including differences in tool use. For example, the chimps at Gombe used sticks to fish for termites and ants, whereas the chimps at Bossou, Guinea, did not. But the Bossou chimps, unlike those in Gombe, used rocks to crack open nuts.

Differences also appeared in grooming behavior. When two chimpanzees groomed each other at Gombe, they frequently grasped an overhead branch with one hand, grooming the other chimp with the free hand. At Mahale, Tanzania, the chimps didn't grasp branches, but held their arms high and clasped hands.

Goodall suggested that these geography-specific behavior patterns were learned and passed down through the generations. They were, that is, *cultural* traditions, just like those found in people of different parts of the world. This was a bold proposal because many scholars held that the capacity for culture is unique to humans. As in the case of toolmaking, Goodall once again challenged the assumption of human uniqueness.

Love and Disillusionment

While Goodall was gaining the trust of the chimpanzees, she was joined by a wildlife photographer, Hugo van Lawick, to document her findings. Goodall and van Lawick fell in love and married in 1964. Two years later Goodall gave birth to their son, whom they also named Hugo. Because the baby was such a messy eater, she nicknamed him Grub, and the nickname stuck.

In order to care for Grub, Goodall stopped following chimps in the forest. When she had time, she worked on scientific reports and administered a growing research staff. She missed the days alone in the forest, but motherhood brought its own rewards, especially the opportunity to see through the eyes of a child.

As time went by, Goodall and van Lawick grew emotionally distant from each other. According to Dale Peterson, a major problem was their differing views on spirituality. Goodall believed in God, which she increasingly viewed as a spiritual power that she felt all around her in the forest. Van Lawick was an atheist.

The issue came to a head in 1972 when young Grub asked his father a question about God. Van Lawick, who was sitting with friends, laughed at the question, and his friends laughed as well. According to Peterson, "This seemed a cruel, almost unforgivable offense to Jane."

A year later Goodall met the new director of Tanzania National Parks, Derek Bryceson. At the time Bryceson was the only white man elected to a government post in Africa. He walked with a cane as a result of a plane crash in World War II, and Goodall considered him to be a very heroic and romantic figure. The two fell in love, and they thought about divorcing their spouses in order to marry. This wasn't an easy decision for Goodall. She worried about the effect on Grub and about Bryceson's ability to cope with separations when she traveled to academic events. According to Peterson, Goodall experienced "great inner turmoil."

In 1974 Goodall and van Lawick divorced, with Goodall maintaining custody of their son. Goodall married Bryceson the next year.

Chimpanzee Violence

Goodall found the early 1970s difficult for another reason. Her research team witnessed lethal violence among the chimpanzees. The chimps split into two groups and engaged in all-out war. The violence shook Goodall. Chimps she had known and loved were killed.

The violence also raised a broader question. Prior to this, Goodall had assumed that chimpanzees were more peaceful than humans. She had believed that humans, who engage in so much violence, had made a wrong turn somewhere; our species had departed from its evolutionary path. But if chimpanzees shared our violent tendencies, our violence seemed to be inherited from our primate past.

On what basis, then, could people hope for peace? If violence was wired into our species' genes, we seemed destined for chaos and evil. Goodall lost much of her faith in a benevolent God who created humans to be kind and peaceful.

During this time of soul-searching, Goodall went to Paris to attend a research conference on the roots of human violence. The trip gave her a chance to visit Notre-Dame Cathedral. When she entered the building, the great Rose Window was glowing in the morning sun. An organ was playing Bach's Toccata and Fugue in D Minor, and the wonderful music filled the vast cathedral. Goodall says that the music "seemed to enter and possess my whole self. It was as though the music itself were alive."

When Goodall thought about the labor that had gone into the cathedral's construction, the thousands of years of worship in it, and this amazing music that came from a human brain, her religious faith reawakened. She thought that all this could not just be chance. There must be a God, a purpose, a human destiny. There must be a guiding power moving us toward a higher, more loving existence.

Goodall didn't conclude that this divine guidance relieves of us the need to make choices. We must work to overcome the violent propensity in our genes. We must work to become loving and caring. But Goodall did conclude that there is a spiritual force aiding us.

Further Tragedies

Unfortunately, the uplifting experience at Notre-Dame couldn't protect her against the events that followed. The war between the two chimpanzee groups continued. It was devastating; in the end, all the members of one entire group—ten in all—were killed. Goliath, who was by then old and frail, was among the victims. The deaths were hard to bear.

What's more, in early 1980 Bryceson was diagnosed with cancer, and he died later that year. During his last weeks, his suffering was intense. Goodall has said these weeks were the most difficult in her life. For a while after his death, Goodall rejected God and found the world to be a bleak place.

Healing in Nature

This time she didn't find healing in a cathedral, but in the forest of Gombe. In her autobiography *Reason for Hope*, Goodall says that one day stands out. She was following several chimps up the slopes, as they moved from one food tree to the next. Suddenly a storm arrived, with loud claps of thunder, lightning, and heavy rain. Goodall and the chimps all found whatever shelter they could. Then, when the sky cleared, the chimps resumed feeding and Goodall became "lost in awe at the beauty around me." She says she "slipped into a state of heightened awareness" that she found difficult to put into words. "Even the mystics," Goodall adds, are unable to describe their brief flashes of spiritual ecstasy. It seemed to me as I struggled afterward to recall the experience, that self was utterly absent: I and the chimpanzees, the earth and trees and air, seemed to merge, to become one with the spirit power of life itself.

She was amazed at the clarity of her sensory perceptions—of the sounds of birds and insects, the patterns of individual leaves, and the scents of damp bark and young, crushed leaves. She said she hadn't been visited by angels, but "I truly believe it was a mystical experience."

Later that day, as she cooked her dinner over a small fire, she thought about ways of trying to understand the world. One way is the window of science. Goodall had worked hard at gaining knowledge through scientific research. But she placed a higher value on the window of the mystics—that of the masters around the world who drew from experiences such as hers that day. Their experiences of awe have informed scriptures, poems, and holy books.

~

Extended Discussion Questioning Goodall's View of Chimpanzee Violence

In 1991, Margaret Power, an anthropologist, challenged Goodall's interpretation of the lethal violence. Whereas Goodall saw the aggression as an innate propensity, Power contended that the fighting wasn't natural. She argued that it was a consequence of a human intervention—the researchers' banana-feeding.

Here is a brief history of the banana-feeding. Although Goodall initially asked her staff to leave bananas for the chimps who came to camp, the practice became problematic. She found that a chimp can eat over fifty bananas at a sitting, so providing them became very costly and difficult. What's more, the bananas lured baboons to the camp, and they often fought with the chimpanzees.

The provisioning also soured the chimpanzees' interactions with one another. Initially the chimps ate the bananas in a relaxed manner. But as more chimps came to camp to get the fruit, hoarding and quarrels arose.

Attempting to solve the problems, Goodall's staff installed boxes that allowed them to regulate access to the bananas. But this didn't work. The closed boxes produced intense frustration in the chimps. Power argued that this frustration caused the aggression that led to the warfare.

Goodall grants that the banana provisioning may have had an impact. But she believes the main cause of the lethal violence was the chimpanzees' natural drive to defend and expand their groups' territories.

Power, in contrast, contends that chimpanzees do not naturally form closed groups that fight over territory. In natural settings, she says, groups are loose-knit, with members coming and going. Power concludes that the lethal fighting was the result of human intervention.

The basic debate—whether chimpanzee violence is natural—continues. In a 2018 book, anthropologist Craig Stanford says that researchers have observed so many instances of chimpanzee violence that most scientists now believe that violence is a natural part of chimpanzee life. But the issue is still open.

A New Direction

In 1986 Goodall's work took a new turn. At a conference she learned that the chimpanzees in Africa were rapidly vanishing, largely because of hunting and logging. She was stunned. The Gombe Reserve, where she worked, was protected from hunting and logging, but most other chimpanzee habitats were not. Goodall says,

> For twenty five years I had lived my dream. I had gloried in the solitude of the forest, learning from some of the most fascinating creatures of our times. Now, with newfound professional confidence, the time had come for me to use the knowledge I had acquired to try to help the chimps in time of need.

So Goodall began touring the globe, giving speech after speech on the plight of the chimpanzees. Since then she has carried her message far and wide.

Goodall also speaks out on the cruel treatment of animals in general. In factory farms, which supply almost all the meat modern humans eat, animals are caged so tightly they can barely move. In response, Goodall has become a vegetarian. Goodall also has written several books and initiated the Roots & Shoots youth programs to help protect the environment and animals. Finally, Goodall speaks out against humans' cruelty toward one another. Until the COVID-19 pandemic hit in 2020, she had been traveling 300 days a year—at age eighty-five.

During her travels, Goodall visited a medical research facility owned by New York University that experimented on animals. There she met the chimp Jo Jo, who had been caged in a standard five by five foot wide, seven foot tall cage for at least ten years. He had lived, Goodall recalls, ten years "of utter boredom interspersed with fear and pain." When she looked into his eyes, she found no hatred in them—"only a sort of gratitude because I had stopped to talk to him, helped to break the grinding monotony of the day." Gently, he groomed the hairs on the back of her wrist.

> Jo Jo had committed no crime, yet he was imprisoned, for life. The shame I felt was because I was human. Very gently, Jo Jo reached out through the bars and touched my cheek where the tears ran down into my mask. He sniffed his finger, looked briefly into my eyes, went on grooming my wrists. I think Saint Francis stood behind us, and he too was weeping.

Concluding Thoughts

Even as a researcher, Goodall retained the spirit of childhood. She maintained her childhood fascination with animals, and she loved to explore the forest with fresh and innocent perceptions.

Goodall also possessed the sense of continuity with nature that seems prominent in childhood. As the classic child psychologists Jean Piaget and Heinz Werner observed, children don't erect boundaries between themselves and the natural world. They assume that all things can think and feel, just like they do. Similarly, Goodall didn't allow boundaries to get in her way. For example, she talked to the mountain peak and the wind as if they could understand her. More fundamentally, she was prepared to find that chimpanzees, like humans, have individual personalities, intelligence, emotions, and the ability to express themselves through a variety of physical gestures. And she concluded that chimps are, in fact, like us in all these ways.

Lacking boundaries between themselves and nature, children sometimes fall into intense, mystical states in which they feel at one with all life and existence. In the preceding chapter, we saw vivid experiences of this kind in the life of Howard Thurman—experiences that shaped his adult view that all life is one.

Unity-of-life experiences, while seemingly less intense, also marked Goodall's childhood. She felt oneness with Beech, her favorite tree, and at age sixteen she wrote a poem about being part of nature. She was developing her feeling of being "part of a great unifying power of some kind."

In adulthood there were at least two occasions when she felt profoundly merged with something much larger than herself. One occasion was her visit to the Notre-Dame Cathedral, where she became lost in the music that filled it. The other time was in the forest, following the death of Bryceson, when she felt at one "with the spirit power of life itself." These two experiences enabled her to get through personal crises, and they confirmed her spiritual view of life.

⇒ 6 ⇐

Rachel Carson

· · · · · · ·

Maintaining Our Childhood
Enthusiasm for Nature

*If I had influence with the good fairy who is sup-
posed to preside over the christening of all children I
should ask that her gift to each child in the world be
a sense of wonder so indestructible that it would last
throughout life . . .*

—Rachel Carson

Rachel Carson is best-known for her 1962 book *Silent
Spring*, which alerted the public to the dangers of pes-
ticides and herbicides. This book presented a frightening
picture. But even in this book, and certainly in her work
as a whole, Carson's goal was more upbeat. She wanted
to promote an appreciation of the beauty and wonder of
the natural world.

Like Thoreau, Carson believed that these positive feel-
ings for nature are strongest in childhood and that, tragi-
cally, children lose these feelings as they grow up. They
become bored, disenchanted adults who are preoccupied

with artificial things. And like Thoreau, Carson wanted to reverse this trend.

In this chapter, we'll first look at Carson's life, touching on some of the themes in her work, and then discuss her thought in more detail.

Carson's Life

Childhood and Education

Rachel Carson (1907–1964) was born in Springdale, Pennsylvania, the youngest of three children, and grew up in a house on sixty-five acres of farmland. Her father tried various business ventures but was never successful. Her mother was a homemaker. The family kept only a few farm animals, but there also were woods and a section of the Allegheny River for Rachel to explore.

Rachel didn't have playmates. Her brother and sister were six and ten years older, and no other children lived nearby. But she regarded the birds and other animals as her friends.

Rachel's mother also loved nature and frequently took Rachel on walks to look for wildlife. The mother was a fan of the nature studies movement of the day. This movement de-emphasized the accumulation of facts; it valued, instead, children's sympathetic feelings toward nature. Rachel would later articulate this educational philosophy with great force.

Even as a child, Rachel wanted to be a writer, and her first stories were about animals. At the age of eight, she wrote a story about two wrens who searched for a home and found a brown house with a green roof. "'Now that is just what we need,' Mr. Wren exclaimed to Jenny, his mate." Her first publication came at age ten, when her story about a World War I airplane battle was accepted by a children's magazine.

Among all aspects of nature, the ocean held her greatest interest. She never saw it as a child, but she thought a great deal about it, imagining what it looked like and what the surf sounded like. In later comments, Carson once spoke as if she, as a child, had been endowed with an innate idea of the sea. She identified with Emily Dickinson, who wrote,

> I never saw a moor,
> I never saw the sea;
> Yet know I how the heather looks,
> And what the sea must be.

Young Rachel did once find a fossilized seashell near her house. She was intrigued. She wondered how it got there, what animal lived in it, and what happened to the sea that was near her house so long ago. She also loved to read stories and poetry about the sea.

Rachel attended two small high schools. Socially, she was rather reserved, but was an outstanding student. After high school, she attended the nearby Pennsylvania College for Women.

College expenses placed a financial burden on her parents, but her mother insisted that she focus solely on her studies and not attempt any campus job. The college emphasized the social graces, but Rachel wasn't interested; she concentrated on her classwork. Intent on becoming a writer, she majored in English, but she also became excited by biology as a way of understanding nature.

As her interest in biology grew, she considered switching her major. This was a difficult decision. During her sophomore year, when she felt discouraged about her writing, she experienced a defining moment. As a thunderstorm raged outside her dormitory room, she read lines from a Tennyson poem in which the protagonist follows the roaring wind to the sea. Carson felt the poem spoke to her in a personal way, suggesting that her own path led to the sea. The poem seemed to tell her that she was on the right track and to pursue her growing interests. The next year she changed her major from English to biology. She enjoyed her courses and won a scholarship to study zoology as an MA student at Johns Hopkins University in Baltimore.

In the summer before she began coursework at Johns Hopkins, she attended a program for future scientists at the Marine Biology Laboratory at Woods Hole on Cape Cod. There, at the age of twenty-two, she saw the ocean for the first time.

A fellow student at Woods Hole remembers that the ocean had a mystical quality for Carson. Carson sometimes wandered off by herself, captivated by all that she experienced. One night, under a full moon, Carson and her friend observed the mating rituals of thousands of small worms just below the surface of the water. Linda Lear, one of Carson's biographers, said Carson "felt united with an ancient time and rite. It was a breathtaking event, one she would watch again and again."

At Woods Hole Carson also first encountered the rich scientific literature on the sea. "But," Carson said, "it is fair to say that my first impressions of the sea were sensory and emotional, and that the intellectual response came later."

Early Career

Carson earned her MA in 1932, at the age of twenty-five. Her thesis was on the embryology of catfish. She then worked toward a PhD at Johns Hopkins, while teaching biology part-time at the University of Maryland's Dental and Pharmacy School. But after she was in the PhD program for a year and a half, the health of her father and her sister Marian deteriorated, and they could no longer provide the family with financial support. To help out, Carson dropped out of her program and picked up additional part-time work at the U.S. Bureau of Fisheries.

At the bureau Carson wrote brochures and radio scripts. Her boss liked her writing and asked her to compose a longer introduction to marine life. She titled it "The World of Waters." This time he rejected her work, saying it wasn't right for the bureau. But with a twinkle in his eye, he added that she should send the essay to the prestigious *Atlantic Monthly* magazine. Carson was delighted by his response, and she put it in a drawer until she could fine-tune it.

Carson's work at the bureau made such a positive impression that in less than two years she was given a full-time position as a government scientist. At the age of twenty-nine, she became one of only two women holding a full-time professional position (positions above the clerical ranks).

A few months later, her sister Marian died. Marian had two daughters, ages eleven and twelve, who needed caretakers. Carson and her mother rented a house and took them in.

Becoming a Prominent Writer

More acutely than ever, Carson felt the need for money and hoped that the sale of her article "The World of Waters" might help. So a year after showing it to her boss, she revised it and submitted it to the *Atlantic Monthly*.

The editors were impressed. They felt Carson gave the general reader a good understanding of scientific findings as well as the beauty and mystery of the sea. The essay was published in 1937 with the new title of "Undersea." Readers did, indeed, respond enthusiastically, and Carson received the standard payment of $100. With this essay, Carson, now thirty years old, had finally pulled her two major interests—science and writing—together.

The essay began by inviting readers to set aside their "human perception of length and breadth and time and place, and enter vicariously into a universe of all-pervading water." The essay also introduced an ecological theme, emphasizing how everything is interrelated. This is true even of the dead animals and plants. Their decomposing bodies rain down minerals and organic matter to the ocean's depths, where they become absorbed into new forms. "Thus, individual elements are lost to view, only to reappear again and again in different incarnations in a kind of immortality."

In 1941, at the age of thirty-four, Carson published her first full book about the sea, *Under the Sea Wind*. The book reads like a novel about the lives of sea animals, but its sales were only modest. Ten years later she published a second book, *The Sea Around Us*, which quickly became a best seller and made Carson a household name.

The Sea Around Us echoed Charles Darwin's emphasis on the extraordinarily long history of the earth. Carson wrote about the eons of time that were required for the formation of the earth's crust, the creation of oceans, and the evolution of life. Many readers wrote to tell her that this immense time span put their personal problems in perspective. Summarizing their thoughts, Carson said that when we think in terms of millions and billions of years, "we are not so impatient that our own problem be solved tomorrow."

The Sea Around Us brought Carson several awards and invitations to give lectures. As a socially reserved person, she was initially reluctant to do this, but friends convinced her to try. She delivered the lectures in a soft voice, but they were eloquent and warmly received.

A Maine Cottage

Earnings from The Sea Around Us eased the problem of supporting her family. The income also enabled her to purchase a cottage on the coast of Maine in 1953, where Carson and her mother spent the summers and falls. The cottage was built on rocks that overlooked the sea, and Carson loved to walk along the beach at low tide, especially early in the morning, when "the world is full of salt smell, and the sound of water, and the softness of fog."

Carson discovered great beauty at the shore, such as the tiny animals called seaflowers—"creatures so exquisitely fashioned that they seemed unreal." She found purple-tinted sand, which under her microscope proved to be "gems, clear as crystal, returning a lovely amethyst light to my eyes."

She speculated that these sand fragments were the end product of a process that began eons ago, when rock particles emerged from deep inside the earth. They were carried thousands of miles, largely by rains and rivers, until they finally came to rest as sand on the beach.

Shortly after Carson and her mother arrived at their cottage, Carson visited their neighbors, Dorothy and Stan Freeman. Carson and Dorothy soon fell in love. They shared happy moments observing nature and exchanged deeply felt letters. Dorothy told Stan about her feelings for Carson, and he said he accepted them. Dorothy Freeman's love provided Carson with support whenever she felt discouraged, and the relationship lasted until Carson's death.

At the Maine cottage, Carson had two special guests, her niece Marjorie and Marjorie's son, Roger. Roger first came to the cottage when he was eighteen months old, and Carson and Roger spent countless hours exploring the woods and seashore together. Roger's fascination with nature impressed her greatly and prompted her to think about how this fascination lives on—or dies out—in adults. Hoping to keep it strong, she wrote an article, "How to Help Your Child Wonder," for the July 1956 issue of the *Woman's Home Companion*.

New Challenges

In 1957, Carson was forty-nine years old and had two projects in mind. One was a book on evolution. The other, which was even more exciting to her, was an expansion of the "Child Wonder" essay into a book. In fact, she sketched out an outline for it and felt that writing it "would be Heaven." But unexpected events intervened.

First, her niece Marjorie, who was often ill, died from pneumonia. Roger was only five years old. Once again, Carson came through for her family; she adopted Roger.

Despite her new childcare responsibilities, Carson undoubtedly would have worked on her book on childhood wonder, but a developing crisis called her away: the growing use of toxic pesticides and herbicides.

Carson had been concerned about the toxic chemicals a decade earlier. She had written to *Reader's Digest* about submitting an article on the dangers of a new "miracle poison," DDT, for destroying insects. But she had received no response. Then, in 1957, new cases of toxic spraying caught her eye. She called government agencies and learned that pesticide use was rapidly expanding.

The following year she read a letter her friend Olga Owens Huckins had written in the *Boston Herald*. Huckins described the effects of mosquito spraying near her home in the small town of Duxbury, Massachusetts. The spray killed seven songbirds immediately. "They were birds," Huckins wrote, "that had lived close to us, trusted us, and built their nests in our trees." The next day a robin dropped suddenly from a branch. Huckins said she was "too heartsick to hunt for other corpses. All of these birds died horribly, and in the same way. Their bills were gaping open, and their splayed claws were drawn up to their breasts in agony."

Carson wanted to write an essay on the poisons and sent proposals to several magazines, but they all turned her down. Many said she was being an alarmist. Finally, she decided to write a book on the subject.

The project was difficult. Carson could not devote herself exclusively to it because of caring for Roger. Then, when she began to make progress, her mother died, which was a shock and painful loss. And when she was about midway through the project, she learned she had breast cancer, and the treatment for the tumor slowed her down.

Finally, she sent the manuscript to the publisher, feeling she had done all she could. It came out in 1962. She titled the book *Silent Spring* because the poisons that killed insects were also killing so many songbirds that spring was becoming eerily quiet.

The book described a wide range of poisons, including nuclear radiation. Carson acknowledged that nature herself produces radiation. But given time—measured in millennia—nature adjusts. In contrast, contemporary humans were producing nuclear radiation and spraying poisons in such great quantities that nature had no time to cope with the onslaught.

On the topic of insecticides and herbicides, Carson wrote,

> sprays, dusts, and aerosols are now applied almost universally to farms, gardens, forests, and homes— nonselective chemicals that have the power to kill every insect, the "good" and the "bad," to still the song of birds and the leaping of fish in the streams, to coat the leaves with a deadly film, and to linger on in soil—all this though the intended target may be only a few weeds or insects. Can anyone believe it is possible to lay down such a barrage of poisons on the surface of the earth without making it unfit for all life? They should not be called "insecticides," but "biocides."

The publication of *Silent Spring* provoked withering attacks, but it also received support. Indeed, the book launched the modern environmental movement.

Carson died of breast cancer in 1964, at the age of fifty-six. Roger was eleven. He went to live with Carson's friend and biographer Paul Brooks and his wife Susie, who became his legal guardians.

Carson never had the opportunity to write the two books she had planned, on evolution and childhood wonder. But let's turn to what she did say on these two topics.

Glimpses into Our Evolutionary Past

Carson observed that while her own fascination with the ocean was particularly intense, many people are attracted to it. They sometimes stand and gaze at it without saying a word. One reason for this attraction, Carson speculated, is that the sea is the ancient "mother of all life." It is where all life began. Perhaps people unconsciously recognize the scene of their far-off ancestry.

Carson added that each of us, like every animal,

> carries in our veins a salty stream in which the elements sodium, potassium, and calcium are contained in almost the same proportions as in sea water. This is our inheritance from the day, untold millions of years ago, when a remote ancestor, having progressed from one-celled to the many-celled stage, first developed a circulatory system in which the fluid was merely water of the sea.

And seawater continues to support the beginning of each of our lives. Each of us begins life "in a miniature ocean" within our mother's womb, and the stages of our embryonic development repeat the steps through which humans evolved, from fish to mammals.

Carson noted that it was a critical event in the history of life when the first sea animals ventured onto land. Many animals developed migratory patterns from sea to land and back to the sea. Today, with luck, we can catch glimpses of this behavior in some very ancient animals.

If we are on a beach in the eastern United States on a May or June night, and the moon is full, we may see the horseshoe crabs move in.

The first to arrive are the males, who wait for the females. The approaching females swim easily in the deeper water but crawl "awkwardly and hesitatingly as the sea shallows beneath them." The females dig in the sand and shed their burdens of eggs; the males fertilize the eggs; and "then the pair moves on, leaving the eggs to the sea, which gently stirs them and packs the sand about them, grain by grain."

The eggs will crack open during the next full moon, for it is ordinarily during the full moon that the tides are sufficiently turbulent to split them. At first the newly hatched crabs will live in shallow bays and sounds. Many won't survive, but those who do will soon make their journey to the depths of the sea. And when they are fully mature, they will themselves return to the shore, under the full moon of a spring night, to deposit and fertilize their eggs.

If we are fortunate enough to watch the crabs emerge from the sea in the moonlight, we may feel a mysterious sense of something almost eternal. "Our thoughts become uncertain; is it really today? or is it a million—or a hundred million years ago?"

Why did sea animals venture onto land in the first place? Scientists can only speculate.

One factor, Carson suggested, had to do with movements of the earth's outer crust. The crust has gradually warped downward and upward, each cycle taking millions of years to complete. These cycles have caused the seas to flood the coastal lands and then retreat. During the Silurian period, 419 to 444 million years ago, the receding seas undoubtedly stranded some animal species in small pools on the shores, some of which lived and endured. Since plant life had already begun colonizing the land, plants may have provided them with a source of food.

Some animals who once lived on land eventually returned to the sea. Fossils indicate that this was true of whales. At one time, Carson speculated, whales were huge land beasts who ventured into shallow waters to feed on marine life. Over the centuries they formed the habit of following the marine life farther and farther into the sea. "Little by little their bodies took on a form more suitable to aquatic life."

Humans evolved from mammals that remained on the land. In evolutionary time, this happened only yesterday. Plants and animals have struggled to survive—in the ocean and on the land—over eons of time, evolving into a spectacular variety of species. Early humans emerged only a few million years ago.

Carson was surprised that many scientists couldn't see that our species is part of this great stream of life and that humans also depend on the environment. In their responses to *Silent Spring*, the scientists spoke as if we are so special that we don't need clean soil, air, and water. For example, scientists admitted that agricultural chemicals could kill thousands of fishes, but they denied that the chemicals could harm the person who drank the water. Carson repeatedly stressed that our species, like all life, is subject to the conditions of the natural environment.

Emotional Responses

Because of our long dependence on the environment, we have evolved emotional responses to it. Carson focused on two emotional responses: our pleasure in nature's beauty and our sense of its mystery.

Beauty. We have already seen how Carson was stirred by nature's beauty, such as the loveliness of the seaflowers in a cove. Carson didn't believe that beauty is a sentiment that people project onto nature. It's part of nature's reality. Referring to *The Sea Around Us*, Carson said, "If there is poetry in my book about the sea, it's not because I deliberately put it there, but because no one could write truthfully about the sea and leave out the poetry." Carson believed nature's beauty is so real that it should be a topic of scientific inquiry.

Not that we must be a scientist to perceive nature's beauty. Humans developed a sensitivity to it as we adapted to our environment. Our pleasure in beauty is part of our "heritage as a living creature."

Mystery. Carson believed that the story of evolution is shrouded in mystery. She recognized that scientists were making discoveries, but she felt, like Einstein, that mysteries will remain because some of nature's secrets lie beyond the reach of the human mind.

When studying nature outdoors, Carson frequently experienced a sense of mystery on a personal, emotional level, as when she watched horseshoe crabs come to shore under the full moon. At times Carson said she felt an "uneasy communication with some universal truth that lies just beyond our grasp."

Carson believed that the biggest scientific mystery is how life began. I have summarized this puzzle and two others in the sidebar.

~

Three Unsolved Mysteries

1. **The Beginning of Life.** How did living proto-
    plasm emerge from inorganic matter? Carson sug-
    gested that in the early ages of the planet, rains
    and weather conditions eroded rocks, allowing salt
    and other minerals to leach into the water. This
    leaching contributed to a mix of ingredients that *set
    the stage* for the emergence of life. But how, precisely,
    did life emerge? Was a spark added to the mix? This
    answer now seems too simple, and the true answer
    continues to elude us.

2. **The Oceans' Depths.** Carson noted that a century
    before she began writing on the sea, people believed
    that the depths of the ocean were lifeless. When
    ships dropped lines very low, they were surprised to
    pull up starfish. Since then, Carson observed, scien-
    tists had discovered numerous new forms of sea life,
    but so much remained unknown that she wondered
    if scientists would ever completely chart the sea
    and its inhabitants. Today, even with technological
    advances, surprisingly little is known.

3. **Migrations.** Carson was amazed by animal migra-
    tions. Animals often travel incredible distances. For
    example, eels from the Chesapeake Bay, as well as
    from Greenland, Belgium, and other parts of the
    world, all migrate to the Sargasso Sea to spawn their
    eggs. Then the eel larvae return to the waters of their
    parents. These larvae are only about half the length
    of the human thumb, yet some travel a thousand

miles "of strange, wild waters without the benefit of chart or compass." How, Carson wondered, do the young eels possibly find their way? The answer continues to elude scientists, as is the case with the migrations of many species of birds and other animals.

Nature's Beauty and Mystery Keep Us Going

Like Thoreau., Carson was concerned about the tensions and weariness that plague our adult lives. She emphasized that nature's beauty can help us immensely. It can bring us "peace and spiritual refreshment."

Carson was extremely upset when real estate developments destroyed woods and highways cut through natural settings like Rock Creek Park in Washington DC, near her Maryland home. Carson urged citizens to protect the "untouched oases of natural beauty [that] remain in the world."

When we attend to nature's beauty, Carson added, we become aware of its refrains—the way the tides continue to ebb and flow, the way each spring brings new flowers and bird migrations. These observations also help us carry on despite disappointments. For "there is something infinitely healing in these repeated refrains of nature—the assurance that dawn comes after night, and spring after winter."

Nature's mystery is of great benefit to us as well. It keeps our curiosity alive. Those who explore nature's mysteries "are never bored" or "weary of life."

Nurturing Wonder—In Children and Ourselves

Carson emphasized that a sense of nature's beauty and mystery is very strong in childhood. As she said, children have a "true instinct for what is beautiful and awe-inspiring." In Carson's case, these emotions continued throughout life. But most children's enchantment with nature fades as they grow up. Concerns with things like money and possessions take over.

Carson said that if a child's enthrallment with nature is to remain strong, it needs early adult support. The child "needs the companionship of at least one adult who can share it, rediscovering with him the joy, excitement, and mystery of the world." Carson had such companionship with her mother.

Carson also had another advantage. She grew up where wild nature was abundant. But for many children this isn't the case. As Carson noted, children increasingly live in artificial environments of concrete and steel. They have little contact with woods, books, and meadows. So even if a caregiver wishes to nurture a child's inborn feelings for nature, it has become difficult to do.

True, parents often try to share nature with children with trips to state and national parks, but considerable parkland is marred by roads and commercial facilities. Similarly, the shore is rarely "wild and unspoiled...It is cluttered with amusement concessions, refreshment stands, fishing shacks—all the untidy litter of what passes under the name of civilization."

Nevertheless, Carson believed there are still opportunities to preserve what is left of nature and to introduce children to it. In her 1956 article, "Help Your Child to Wonder, " Carson addressed parents' widespread sense of inadequacy as teachers. "How can I possibly teach my child about nature?" parents ask. "Why, I don't even know one bird from another!"

Carson's response was that "for the child, and for the parent seeking to guide him, it is not half so important to *know* as to *feel*." Once children's senses and emotions are aroused—once they experience nature's beauty and become excited by the new and unknown—they will naturally want to learn more and will acquire facts.

What is most important for us as parents, then, is to share our enthusiasm with children. And to do this, we need to become like children again. We need to let wonder back into our lives.

Carson recommended that we walk outside with children and become receptive to all that is around us—the wind, birdcalls, the stars, moving clouds. She suggested one way to experience unnoticed beauty is to ask ourselves, "What if I had never seen this before?" We can then share our delight with a child, even if we don't know the names of the things we are observing. We "can still drink in the beauty, and think and wonder at the meaning of what [we] see."

Carson illustrated her approach through her outdoor walks in Maine with her grandnephew Roger, which began when he was twenty months old. Often, she took Roger outside at night, when there is a special magic in the air. Sometimes they just felt the mist from the sea; sometimes they searched for insects that were producing their symphonies of sound; sometimes they focused binoculars on the moon and watched to see what birds migrated across it.

At night, when we cannot see so well, we rely more on hearing and come to appreciate sounds more than we otherwise might. One sound that haunted her and Roger was that of an insect she called the "fairy bell-ringer." She and Roger never saw it. She added that "I'm not sure I want to. His voice—and surely he himself—is so ethereal, so delicate, so otherworldly, that he should remain invisible." Carson said that the faint sound is exactly what one would expect to come from the "bell held in the hand of the tiniest elf, inexpressibly clear and silvery."

Carson made no conscious effort to name plants or animals for Roger. She just expressed her own pleasure in what they discovered. Later she was amazed by the extent to which Roger had somehow picked up names. Even at only one and a half, he identified shells as "winkies" (periwinkles) and "weks" (whelks), "without my knowing quite how this came about, for I never tried to teach him."

In a similar vein, Carson argued that science education in the schools initially should encourage students' *feelings* for nature. Teachers should start by taking students to forests, fields, and the seashore, where they can observe animals living freely in their natural habitats. Students will then have a chance to sense the beautiful intricacies and wonder of life. If, instead, students are primarily exposed to animals in laboratories, it will be difficult for them to form these impressions.

In support of her educational position, Carson noted that "some of the most gifted and imaginative biologists have initially approached their subject through the medium of sensory impression and emotional response." Carson didn't cite specific biologists, but many pioneering biologists, including Darwin, Goodall, Konrad Lorenz, and Marshall Nirenberg (who helped crack the genetic code), loved nature as children and maintained their emotional connection to it as adults.

Concluding Thoughts

As we have seen, Carson wanted to convince us that our enchantment with nature can counteract the boredom and disillusionments of adult life. Carson also believed that our enthusiasm for nature has a wider benefit. It is important for the planet itself.

Carson was appalled by the damage humans have inflicted on the earth. Humans, she said, have become intoxicated with their own power to bend nature to their will, and they will surely end up destroying themselves and the world.

Carson saw no single remedy for "this unhappy trend"—no panacea. But she said that if we can appreciate the beauty and wonder of the world, we will acquire greater humility and have less taste for destruction.

On a happier note, Carson concluded her essay on childhood wonder by recounting a letter she had received. It came from a woman who wanted advice on choosing a vacation spot. The woman said she had loved the seashore all her life but could no longer climb the rocky shores of Maine. She was eighty-nine years old. Carson said that as she put the letter down, she was warmed by the "fires of wonder" that "still burned brightly" in this woman, just as these fires must have burned when the woman was a child. The woman, like Carson, had remained forever young.

⸙ 7 ⸙

Conclusion

When I selected the six biographies for this book, I thought that each would illustrate the adult use of one specific childhood power. For example, I chose Thoreau to exemplify the use of fresh senses. But as I delved into the life histories, I saw that most of the individuals I had chosen exercised more childhood strengths than I anticipated. A quick glance at the table below reveals that most drew upon two or three childhood powers.

Childhood Powers Evident in Adult Lives

Childhood power	Thoreau	Einstein	Brontë	Thurman	Goodall	Carson
Fresh senses	√				√	√
Curiosity, wonder, mystery, beauty	√	√	√		√	√
Play		√	√			
Sense of unity of life	√			√	√	

Nevertheless, I found that a specific childhood strength was pivotal in each life.

The Pivotal Childhood Powers in the Six Lives

Fresh Senses

As I anticipated, reviving fresh senses was pivotal in the life of **Henry David Thoreau**. When he was able to recapture the innocent outlook of childhood, he experienced the wonder and beauty of nature and was uplifted. As he said, "To perceive freshly, with fresh senses, is to be inspired." Thoreau felt that the fresh perception of nature can liberate people from the dreariness of life.

As I noted in chapter 1, in Thoreau's day the call for fresh perception was beginning to be heard in the art world as well. It emerged in the movement known as Impressionism. Over a half-century later, fresh perception became the goal of the philosophical school of phenomenology. Led by Edmund Husserl, phenomenological philosophers said that we see clearly only if we suspend our expectations, judgments, and preconceived ideas and encounter the world just as it presents itself to us. As Husserl put it, we need to return "to the things themselves."

But Husserl and most of his followers wrote in very abstract language and were difficult to understand. They also neglected the way children demonstrate the approach they advocated. To an extent, psychologists Abraham Maslow and Ernest Schachtel made the phenomenological approach clearer, while observing that it is dominant in children. But the first person to bring fresh, childlike perception to life was Thoreau. He described his immediate perceptions of birdsong, sunlight, wind, night sounds—of all his natural surroundings.

Curiosity, Wonder, Mystery & Beauty

These emotions appeared in the biographies as a cluster. The individuals who spoke about one of the emotions frequently mentioned the others as well. They seemed to regard them as highly interrelated.

These emotions were of central importance to **Albert Einstein**. Despite his brilliance, he had to exert superhuman effort to develop his new theories, and in this he was driven by the passionate curiosity he retained from childhood.

Ironically, Einstein suggested that the physicist's passionate curiosity is intensified by a human limitation. The human mind can understand the universe's beautiful laws only imperfectly, so the laws are shrouded in mystery. This mystery creates a powerful allure, stimulating physicists' efforts to learn more about the laws even though progress is slow. Glimpses attract the scientist like the elusive sirens in ancient mythology.

The sense of wonder, beauty, and related emotions also were of paramount importance to **Rachel Carson.** Carson didn't expose the effects of pesticides and poisons in order to tell a grim story. Instead, she wrote out of a love of nature. She wanted people to appreciate nature's beauty and mystery. She felt that they would then have less taste for nature's destruction.

Like Einstein, Carson believed that these precious emotions were strongest in childhood. Children, she said, have a "true instinct for what is beautiful and awe-inspiring." She wanted adults to nurture this instinct so it would continue to be strong in adulthood.

Although most the individuals in this book were enthralled by nature, Carson differed in one respect: she was stirred by the mysteries of the distant past. When, for example, she watched horseshoe crabs swim from the ocean onto land under a full moon, just as they had done through eons of time, she felt as if she was in a magical time zone. Was it really today? Or was it a hundred million years ago?

Does this feeling for the mystery of the past begin in childhood? I can only answer on the basis of my own memories. I had strong feelings at the ocean, but I had clearer impressions of stones. At the age of seven or so, I picked up stones that I thought must possess secret, ancient knowledge because they looked so old. No one told me stones were very old; they just struck me that way. I remember feeling that my thoughts would sound strange to others, so I didn't share them with anyone. In chapter 10, I will discuss the value that stones can have for us.

Thoreau also prized feelings of wonder, mystery, and beauty. He felt that they are nature's gifts to us. But he believed our primary task is to recover the fresh perceptions of childhood. Only then will nature's enchantment come to us.

Play

The life of **Charlotte Brontë** illustrates the enormous creative power of make-believe play. Her play, frequently conducted with her siblings, fueled her imagination and led to great works of literature. Moreover, her imagination provided relief from terrible sadness. As she put it, "The faculty of imagination lifted me when I was sinking."

I recognize that Brontë is not a typical example. Few children engage in such intense play with their siblings and continue this cooperative play well after childhood. We might say that Brontë received ongoing support from a family play network.

At the same time, Brontë's unusual situation should not distract us from the power of play in ordinary children. Between about two and seven years of age, the urge to play emerges with tremendous force and appears in circumstances where we wouldn't expect it. Based on her pediatric experience, my wife Ellen tells me that young children commonly play with equipment in the emergency room despite illnesses. George Eisen has documented how childhood play even emerged in the ghettos and concentration camps of the Holocaust. Eisen says, "Play burst forth spontaneously and uncontrollably without regard to the external situation."

And while the imaginative quality of play typically subsides after the age of seven or eight, it is sustained or revived in a range of creative individuals, including artists, novelists, and scientists. As Erik Erikson suggested, **Einstein's** imaginative thinking had its origins in childhood play. Although Einstein himself wrote that the driving force behind his work was his childlike curiosity and sense of mystery, his playful imagination was certainly important.

Unity of Life

A childhood feeling of the unity of life had a profound effect on **Howard Thurman**. Especially when he was at the seashore as a boy, he felt the sand, sea, stars, and night were one lung through which all breathed—and he was part of it. This experience of the unity of life undergirded his belief that people of different racial backgrounds can overcome any differences, for they are all part of something much greater.

A sense of continuity with nature has been central to the research of **Jane Goodall**. Prepared to see chimpanzees as similar to humans, she described how they, like us, have cognitive abilities, personalities, and emotions. Moreover, Goodall's heightened experiences of oneness with nature affirmed her belief in an all-pervasive spiritual power. This feeling helped her to emotionally recover from the death of her husband Derek Bryceson.

The idea of an all-pervasive spiritual presence has appeared in a variety of cultural and historical contexts. The poet William Wordsworth wrote about this spiritual presence, as did Emerson and the Transcendentalists. Native American and Eastern philosophies have referred to something similar.

In his classic book *The Varieties of Religious Experience*, William James described such unity-of-life experiences under the heading of Mysticism. James noted that mystical experiences come to people unannounced, as if they have a will of their own. James also observed that the most powerful mystical experiences usually take place when people are in natural settings.

James described unity-of-life experiences primarily in adults, but in a pioneering essay, Edith Cobb proposed that they are more likely to occur in childhood. In support of Cobb, nature educator David Sobel has called attention to two collections of mystical or spiritual experiences. These accounts were in response to newspaper queries that invited readers to send in their personal stories. Many readers told about unity-of-life experiences and said these experiences were most common in childhood.

I strongly suspect larger, more systematic surveys will confirm that childhood is, indeed, the time when unity-of-life experiences dominate. Curiously though, we have encountered two exceptions in this book. In the lives of

Thoreau and Goodall, the most intense experiences of this kind occurred when they were adults. Why?

It seems that although children, compared to adults, are naturally more open to these experiences, there is another variable at work: *being alone*. Thurman felt lonely as a boy when nature comforted him; Goodall was alone, without her husband, when she had her intense experience in the forest; Thoreau was wondering whether he could live alone at Walden Pond when nature befriended him. Being alone played a role in each case.

True, it doesn't seem that solitude is *necessary* for *all* mystical experiences. In one of his several experiences, Thurman was on a ship with his wife. But a variety of evidence points to the *importance* of being alone. In autobiographies studied by psychologist Louise Chawla, nearly all the writers described their childhood unity-of-life experiences as taking place in solitude. Similarly, the anecdotes collected by James and those cited by Sobel suggest that people are most receptive to these experiences when social life is in abeyance.

This is not to suggest that mystical experiences are merely the fantasies of lonely people. Yes, people may be more receptive to them when they are alone. But the message of the experiences—that all life is one—is correct. Modern biology has repeatedly underscored this fact. Investigators have found that all life-forms use the same genetic code and create proteins from the same amino acids. Recent research on genomes (organisms' total DNA) has revealed amazing similarities across species. When individuals have a mystical sense of the unity of life, they encounter a basic truth.

☞ *Part II* ☜

How Do We Follow Their Lead?

That's the wise thrush: he sings each song twice over
Lest you should think he never could re-capture
The first fine careless rapture!
                                        —Robert Browning

⇒ 8 ⇐

Perceiving Nature
with Fresh Senses

"Wake up and smell the roses!"

—Anonymous advice

Thoreau urged us, as adults, to recapture our childhood perceptions of nature. He said if we perceive nature with fresh senses, we will open ourselves to nature's wonder and beauty. After Thoreau, several naturalists—people who love to study nature—also have encouraged fresh, childlike perception. These naturalists include Rachel Carson, Cathy Johnson, and Joseph Cornell.

The specific recommendations by Thoreau and other naturalists frequently overlap. They have become a common toolbox for expanding our awareness of our natural surroundings. I will summarize those I have found especially worthwhile.

Let Your Mind Go

Find an outdoor spot you enjoy, such as a backyard, park, beach, or woodland. If possible, the setting should be away from traffic. Go there alone, turn off your smartphone, and sit or stand quietly. Then let your mind go—ignoring your thoughts—and receive impressions just as they come to you. You might hear breezes rustling bushes or feel mist on your face. You might hear one or more birds. Perhaps you are struck by patterns of sunlight.

It's good to be patient, to take the time needed to become fully aware of your impressions. If you hear a bird singing, let yourself take it in fully. You might become increasingly impressed by the song's beauty or find that it lifts your spirits.

Make no effort to name things or think of explanations for them. If you see an unfamiliar plant or animal, you can look it up in a book later—not now. For now, your goal is to let your mind go and be aware of nature's immediate sensations.

Ask Rachel Carson's Question

Carson recognized that adults have difficulty perceiving the world freshly—to notice things anew. One of her recommendations was to ask ourselves, "What if I had never seen this before?" Asking this question helps us become like a child again because the child perceives so much for the first time.

I tried this one afternoon where I live, on our farm sanctuary in rural, upstate New York. It was late winter, and the snow was melting, filling the waterways. As I walked on a dirt road, I stopped by a stream running into a pipe that allowed it to cross under the road. Thinking about Carson's question, I asked myself, *What if I was coming across this for the first time?* I was suddenly struck by the force and loudness of the water as it rushed into the pipe. I was surprised that it never seemed so loud before.

The next day I looked at a tree near the same road and asked myself Carson's question again. I had never paid much attention to the tree before. This time, imagining seeing it for the first time, I was struck how branches rose from the trunk in a way that formed a beautiful pattern. They seemed to weave together in lovely harmony.

These and other experiences lead me to believe that Carson's question can work for you. It can enable you to perceive the world in a new way.

Close Your Eyes

Because humans generally rely so strongly on one sense—vision—you can perceive the world freshly simply by closing your eyes. I have found that when I stand quietly and shut my eyes, sounds become louder and sharper. I hear birdsong much more clearly. I also become aware of the sounds of the breezes and their cool feeling. To my surprise, I become much calmer inside and feel as if I am being enveloped by nature.

I have asked several people who work at our farm sanctuary to engage in this exercise—to stand quietly for a minute or so with eyes closed—and they have independently reported the same impressions. I asked one person why she thought she felt calmer, and she said, "I think shutting your eyes in nature quiets the mind."

Closing our eyes allows us to become more acutely aware of how things feel to our hands. It is interesting to touch the bark of a tree with one's eyes closed. Similarly, we can better focus on aromas and tastes of plants with eyes closed. The world opens to us in new ways.

Walk off the Beaten Path

Thoreau emphasized the need to get outside routine or conventional outlooks. He found that he couldn't achieve this experience when he walked on well-traveled roads. When, for example, he walked on the main road to town, he found that his thoughts were about the town— not his unexplored surroundings.

So Thoreau got off the roads and meandered about in meadows and woods without any destination or schedule in mind. Then his senses were open to subtle things like a cluster of weeds he hadn't previously noticed. Once he looked at them, he was struck by their beauty.

A naturalist who is especially enthusiastic about walking off the beaten path is Cathy Johnson. She even recommends taking chances on becoming lost. As far as I know, Thoreau's advice wasn't this extreme.

Take a Night Walk

Thoreau found that he could get outside his routine experience by going outdoors at night. Sounds, in particular, became louder. In rural areas, even when walking on a familiar road, sensations like a moving branch or a sudden gust of wind can seem a bit frightening—the way the world often seems to the child. It can be a bit scary, but also fun and exciting.

New experiences can also occur when going outdoors in the early morning or late evening. Watching a sunrise or sunset can affect us in new and moving ways.

Try New Positions

You can open yourself to the world in new ways by taking new physical positions. Lie on your back in the grass. You will probably gain a new perspective on the sunlight and objects like treetops. While lying on your back, look at the clouds or the stars like you might have as a child.

Go Barefoot

Going barefoot is also something you might have done as a child. Walking without shoes opens the soles of your feet to sensations like mud, grass, and sand. It also will sometimes give you a vague feeling of connection to something much larger beneath your feet.

Take a Walk with a Child

Carson's goal was to encourage the child's sense of wonder, and to do this it helps to share in the child's wonder. For example, if the child shows enthusiasm at the sight of the moon, take a moment to appreciate it, too. You don't need to say much; the child can sense your shared enthusiasm.

As a specific strategy, take a walk with a toddler (a one- or two-year-old), letting the child take the lead. The toddler typically walks with no destination in mind, just enjoying the walk, stopping to examine objects that catch her eye—a leaf, a worm, a puddle of water. Each object is a source of fascination. If you can see the world like the toddler does, enchantment will reenter your life.

Write Poetry

One way to hold on to our immediate sensory impressions is to write about them later in the day. Poetry is particularly useful for recapturing sensory impressions. Consider the following lines by Gary Snyder.

> Ah to be alive
>   on a mid-September morn
>   fording a stream
>   barefoot, pants rolled up . . .

Rustle and shimmer of icy creek waters
Stones turn underfoot, small and hard as toes
    cold nose dripping
    singing inside
    creek music, heart music,
    smell of sun on gravel

We can almost feel the cold, sunshine, and stones under our bare feet.

Your poems don't have to be great to help you retain your sensory impressions. What's more, they will make you more alert to new sensory impressions the next time you are out of doors.

Most Important: Stay Open and Receptive

I have listed a variety of strategies for recovering the fresh and unexpected sensations of childhood. But more important than any particular strategy is your mental attitude—your openness and receptivity to nature around you. If you have this attitude, you will experience the world anew.

≈ 9 ≈

Recovering Play

*And forget not that the earth delights to feel your
bare feet and the winds long to play with your hair.*

—Kahlil Gibran

For adults who wish to bring more joy into their lives,
a good starting point is Stuart Brown's book *Play*.
Too frequently, Brown notes, we are caught up in hectic,
high-pressured lives and feel a chronic sadness. As Thoreau put it, "The mass of men lead lives of quiet desperation." Brown says play reinvigorates us.

Brown defines play as a state of mind that can occur
during any activity. When we are at play, we do things
for the love of the activity itself. Play can even occur at
work. When work is most fulfilling, it feels like play.

Here is a list of recommendations I have drawn from
Brown's book.

Stuart Brown's Recommendations

1. First and foremost, recognize the value of play. Our
    society generally trivializes play, making us feel that
    we should always be serious. But when we play, we
    are happy and creative.

2. Think about what you did as a child that gave you "unfettered pleasure." Was it drawing? Sewing? Playing basketball? Gardening? Think of what you can do to bring back that playful feeling.

3. Take vacations. They can be fun and relaxing and give us new energy when we return from them.

4. Bring play and humor into relationships. When relationships feel too serious or tired, playful interactions lighten and enliven them.

5. Joke around at work. Humor and laughter help us get through difficult jobs. And a playful attitude at work can lead to valuable innovation.

6. If you feel stuck, move around physically. Take a walk. Run, skip, jump, or dance. Our first play as a child was physical, and movement can get us started playing again.

7. If you feel stuck, it also helps to play with a pet.

Play with Children

I have found that a good way of recovering play in one's life is to play with children.

Play with Babies

If there is a new baby in your life, an exhilarating experience awaits you. Beginning at about two months of age, the baby will gaze into your eyes and smile. If you let yourself respond in ways that feel natural, the two of you will interact in playful ways that will light up your life.

With the aid of frame-by-frame film analyses, Daniel Stern has documented these happy exchanges. In one film segment, a three-month-old baby finished nursing and looked up at his mother with a broadening smile. She said, "Well, hello!...heelo...heeelloooo," her pitch rising. Stern reported that "with each phrase, the baby expressed more pleasure." The interaction subsided a moment; then the baby lurched forward with a fuller smile. The mother reciprocated, and they began an "I'm gonna tickle you" game that both enjoyed.

Stern observes that such play occurs in many cultures and that we, as adults, use a high-pitched voice and gestures that are much like those of the baby. We seem to lose ourselves in pleasurable, infant-like states.

Vicariously Enjoy Toddlers' Independent Mastery

Caregivers, then, have a natural opportunity to get off to a playful start with infants. But when infants reach about one year old, caregivers usually become more serious. Babies, who are now toddlers, begin to walk and try out exciting activities such as stair climbing and jumping, and caregivers worry about the children's safety. They issue instructions like "Be careful...Don't climb like that...Let me show you."

Toddlers aren't happy with the adults' interventions. They want to do things on their own.

You can respect toddlers' wish for independence and still ensure their safety. When they try out new activities such as climbing and jumping, stand by unobtrusively, keeping a watchful eye while giving them the freedom to act on their own. As you watch your youngster, you will vicariously enjoy her efforts at independent mastery.

Give the Child the Power Position

The period of intense independence usually lasts just a few months. At the age of one and a half or so, children begin to enjoy our participation in their play. This is true of rough-and-tumble play, which includes physical play such as wrestling, chasing, and King of the Mountain games.

When you wrestle with a young child, roll over on your back so the child can get on top, in the power position. You may do this without even thinking about it; it comes naturally. Children love being in this position. Sometimes more than one child climbs on. As the wrestling goes on, they frequently laugh with such glee that it can become great fun for you as well.

Rough-and-tumble play, which begins in the toddler years, usually continues into the late elementary school years (until about age eleven). It also occurs among the youngsters in many other species, including chimpanzees, dogs, and wolves. And in these species, too, adults wrestle with the young ones and let them assume the dominant positions. Scientists who study animal behavior call this "role reversal."

You also can give the child a superior advantage in chase games. Although you might be able to run faster than a child, act as if you are slower. Children find it fun and exciting when you cannot run fast enough to catch them. Similarly, children often think it is hilarious when you claim, "I'm too fast; you'll never catch me," and then run so clumsily you are easy to catch.

There are many spur-of-the-moment opportunities to put a child in the superior position. I recently entered a shopping center, and saw a boy, who later told me he was nine, trying to walk on a narrow, six-inch-tall ledge. He maintained his balance for four or five steps, but then lost it and jumped off. I asked him if I could try and acted as if I could only take one step before falling off. "How do I do this?" I asked. With obvious pleasure he began giving me directions. It was an exciting—and probably new—opportunity to supervise an adult.

Another occasion arose when our four grandsons were between four and nine years old. They were rambunctious boys who received frequent time-outs. One evening I began to tell them a ghost story when their father called out from the next room, "No scary stories allowed; they get bad dreams."

The oldest boy laughed and joked: "You have to have a time-out, Grandpa." I pretended to mope and asked what a time-out meant. The boys eagerly explained the rules. I had to sit perfectly quiet for three minutes or I'd get an extended sentence. I did what they said, violating the rules on occasion and receiving longer punishments. Sometimes I pleaded for exemptions, which they denied.

Being in charge of my punishment gave them enormous pleasure, and they looked for every opportunity to assign me more time-outs. Although I consistently pretended to suffer from their orders, inwardly I found the episodes to be very fun.

Participate in Make-Believe Play

From about two to seven years old, children engage in considerable make-believe play. They use props such as sticks, stones, dirt, and dolls to make up dramas. They enjoy our participation, happily assigning us roles like the customers in a fantasy bake shop. Some scholars have suggested that adults initiate this play. Elsewhere, I have disagreed; I believe the initiative typically comes from the child. In any case, the play experience is more pleasurable for children if we, as adults, allow them to take charge of the action. And as we become players in the dramas they weave, we regain the happy feelings that we had in our own childhoods.

Participate in Informal Games

At the age of seven or so, children become interested in competitive sports with rules, like baseball and soccer. Today's adults have taken charge of the children's play through organizations like Little League and youth soccer. These adult-structured sports become very serious matters for both adults and children. The games lose their fun. They aren't playful.

Try playing the sports with children in informal ways, putting the emphasis on the fun. You might suggest kids play baseball with you pitching a soft ball very slowly, so they all have a chance to hit successfully. Or just play catch or kick a soccer ball around. Or organize games like hide-and-seek, capture the flag, or hopscotch. Purposely handicap your play so the kids dominate. If you are like me, you will feel these informal games to be lots of fun.

Video Games?

Today, video games have become part of many adult lives. But as Brown observes, they present problems. They can be socially isolating. People become preoccupied with their games to the exclusion of other people. True, video games increasingly involve multiple players who interact, but social isolation is something to bear in mind.

I have long been concerned about another problem that Brown mentions. Video games remove people from the natural world. People playing the games are focused on screens. They don't experience the sensations of hiking on a windy day, riding ocean waves, climbing trees, or digging in dirt. They don't feel the excitement of discovering insects or small animals in vacant lots, or the beautiful patterns of clouds when resting on their backs on the grass. Such experiences were common in children's traditional outdoor play, and many of them are still available to us as adults.

≈ 10 ≈

Connecting with Nature

·······

Stone Meditations

Stones bear a hidden message for those who read with their hearts.
—John (Fire) Lame Deer, Lakota elder

We have seen how Thurman, Thoreau, and Goodall had intense, mystical experiences in which they felt at one with nature. We might want to have such experiences ourselves and therefore spend time in natural settings waiting for them. But they seem to come on their own accord and cannot be rushed. What additional approaches, then, might deepen our connection with nature?

One is through stones.

My own interest in stones began in my childhood. I was fascinated by them. Whenever I have mentioned this in public talks, people have told me that they, too, were intrigued by stones as children and, moreover, they are still drawn to them.

Some stones seem to immediately attract us. Then, as we examine them, we see aspects of ourselves—or qualities we would like to have in them. Stones become like our teachers, providing us with self-awareness. And as we learn from them, our connection to them grows.

The effect of stones is somewhat mysterious. Perhaps they are like the ocean in that way. As Carson said, when we look at the ocean, we may have a dim sense that she is where life began. It is as if we are looking at our origins. Stones, too, go back to the beginnings of life. The oceans needed rock and stone erosion to create the brine—the salty seawater—that hosted the first living things. So we may intuitively sense that stones have something to do with where we came from.

Several years ago, I began bringing baskets of stones into my college classes. I invited the students to pick one that attracted them, and I asked questions that might help them think about them. I also talked to friends about how they felt about stones. From these sources, I developed my "stone meditation recommendations." Let's first look at my suggestions for stone meditations for individuals. Then I will describe group experiences.

Individual Meditations

1. As you walk in parks or on beaches, gravel roads, or nature trails, occasionally pick up a stone you like. Choose stones that are small enough to hold in your hand or put in your pocket.

2. After you've gathered four or five stones, find a quiet moment to look them over. Select one that is particularly appealing.

3. Hold the stone a minute or two. Rub it. Inspect it. Get to know it.

4. Ask yourself, "What attracted me to this particular stone?"

5. Think: "Does my choice of this stone have anything to do with what I value in life? Does it have to do with who I am as a person?

   People are attracted to their stones for a variety of reasons. Some are drawn to craggy, complex stones because they feel that way inside. They are trying to understand themselves and sort things out. Others like a stone that is shiny on a visible surface and rougher elsewhere, observing that this is how they feel about themselves.

   Some like stones that are very solid because they feel they are solid, or wish they were. Others are attracted to stones that are shiny and say, "I like beautiful things." Others who select shiny stones resist using jewelry but wish they could. For them, the stone represents how they'd like to be. The variations are enormous.

6. Does the stone bring back any childhood memory?

7. Consider the fact that your stone is very old— probably millions of years and perhaps even billions of years old. Think, "If this stone could talk, what might it say to me?"

8. Ask yourself: "How do I feel about this stone now?"

Group Experiences

Try also to engage in a stone meditation with a group. It can be with a gathering of friends, a club, or other organization. If you are a teacher, you can lead a meditation with your class. Group experiences can be richer than individual meditations. Groups can also add a spirit of community that supports people's feelings about stones.

Gathering the Stones. Prior to the group experience, an individual or individuals collect small stones. Each should have a unique shape and color. A few might contain quartz. The stones will vary in size, but as with the individual exercise, all the stones should fit comfortably in one's pocket or the palm of one's hand.

The Moderator. The group selects a moderator. This individual doesn't take charge of the discussion. The moderator simply passes around the bowl of stones and then asks the questions listed below. The moderator should make sure everyone who wishes to respond has time to do so.

1. The moderator says: *I'm passing around a bowl of stones. Take one that appeals to you.*

    In a minute I will ask you questions. Please don't comment on another person's answer. Each answer is true for each person. Just listen fully to what each person says.

    As moderator, my task is to ask questions and listen. I will not participate in the experience myself, although after we have finished, I may share a few thoughts.

2. After everyone has a selected a stone, the moderator says: *Hold your stone a minute or so. Inspect it, rub it if you want to. Get to know it.*

3. *Why did you select the stone you did? What attracted you to it? Who would like to begin?*

   Individuals take turns talking about their preferences. As each person completes a comment, the moderator nods and says: *Thank you.*

   On occasion a participant spontaneously says how the choice of a stone relates to her or his personality. That's fine. The next question gives everyone a chance to think about this.

4. *Do you feel your choice has anything to do with what you value or who you are as a person?*

5. After everyone has had a chance to talk about his or her stone, ask: *Does the stone bring back a childhood memory for anyone?*

   In my experience, about a third of the people share memories. Their memories, like their reasons for selecting stones, vary widely. Some memories are happy, some are sad. Some are associated with losses. In my college classes, there are usually a few international students for whom the stones evoke memories of their homelands.

6. *How old would you guess your stone is?*

7. After people have speculated a minute or so, say: *You are holding something extremely ancient.*

Some stones are actually a billion years old. In parts of Wisconsin and elsewhere, there are stones that are three or four billion years old. Some of these come from a time before life appeared on the planet. Most stones are much older than our own species, which seems to have branched off from other primates about six million years ago.

If your stone could talk, it could tell you things about the history of the earth that we can only speculate about.

8. Close with an anecdote:

The Swedish landscape architect Patrik Grahn reports that patients hospitalized with medical and emotional problems often find comfort in the stones they pick up during walks on rural hospital grounds. They find inspiration in the stones' ability to endure through the ages, despite all the environmental assaults the stones have experienced. In addition, the extraordinary age of the stones helps patients view their current problems as less overwhelming in the grand scheme of things.

With a group of five to fifteen or so, the exercise usually lasts thirty minutes.

When it is over, people may say things such as: "I feel very close to my stone" and "I never thought I would respect a stone." Some want to take their stones home with them.

For Further Reading on Stones

Carl Jung, *Memories, Dreams, Reflections* (New York: Basic Books, 1961). In this autobiography, the psychoanalyst described the role that stones played in his adult life. A critical episode occurred soon after he and Sigmund

Freud parted ways. Jung felt disoriented and disconnected from himself. It was as if he were suspended in midair; he couldn't get in touch with his inner life. Then he had a memory of his passionate play with stones as a child. He wanted to reexperience this passion, and even though he felt it was childish, he began building things with stones once again. His play released a stream of fantasies and led to an exploration of the forces in his unconscious mind—forces which, he concluded, are shared worldwide. (See especially chapters 6 and 8 of Jung's book.)

M. Bjornerud, *Reading the Rocks: The Autobiography of the Earth* (New York: Basic Books, 2005). An introduction to the topic.

John (Fire) Lame Deer and Richard Erdoes, *Lame Deer: Seeker of Visions* (New York: Simon & Schuster, 1994). Lame Deer, a Lakota elder and healer, told how his people identified stones with the ancient spiritual world and how they used stones in their healing ceremonies.

William Crain, "Stones," *Encounter: Education for Meaning and Social Justice* (Autumn, 2007). A summary of how Jung and others found stones helpful in their lives.

Going Forward

I have reviewed the lives of six people who have drawn upon the strengths of childhood, and I have suggested some ways of recapturing these qualities ourselves. I hope that I have given you much to think about and have provided jumping-off points for your own thoughts. Have memories of your own childhood emerged through this discussion? Do you recall instances of wonder in your first encounters with objects? Have you considered regaining the fresh outlook of the child? Do you see the need to become more playful? What ideas do you have for achieving this?

I have introduced stone meditations as a way of reconnecting with nature. Are you personally interested in stones, and have they contributed to your feelings for nature? Perhaps you are more interested in other aspects of the natural world such as animals, trees, or the ocean. Has your time with them changed you in any way? Have you experienced the deep peacefulness of nature or being at one with all life?

Each of us has had a unique childhood and has particular needs as an adult. So there can be no standard recipe for reviving the powers of childhood. We must each find our own way.

Appendix A

· · · · · · ·

The Child as Guide:
A Brief History

Genius is childhood recaptured.
—Charles Baudelaire

The notion that adults should value childhood qualities isn't common, but it is very old. Lao Tzu, the ancient Chinese Taoist, said the wise person shares the child's open trust. Jesus told his disciples that people must become humble like children to enter heaven.

A Poet's Vision

In the late eighteenth and early nineteenth century, the poet William Wordsworth praised the child's special attunement to nature. In his autobiographical poem "The Prelude," Wordsworth described how his feelings for nature developed. Growing up in England's Lake District, he was sometimes frightened by nature, but more often he experienced delight and comfort in it. He felt that a "gracious spirit" permeated his natural surroundings—the trees, cliffs, and waters—and he felt this spirit in himself as well. This feeling of unity with nature gave him a wonderful sense of calm. Such impressions were strongest in his childhood.

Wordsworth's mother died when he was seven years old, and his father, when he was thirteen. As an adult, he experienced other losses and disappointments. A romantic relationship ended badly, and he grieved over the drowning of a brother. He also was deeply disillusioned by the chaos and repression that followed the French Revolution. But his strong early attachment to nature, as well as his later feelings for it, helped sustain him. He continued to delight in nature's beauty and to feel its soothing presence.

Wordsworth's most widely read poem is his 1807 "Ode to Immortality." In it, he said that children, coming directly from God, see heaven's presence in their natural surroundings. Wordsworth opened his poem with the lines,

> There was a time when meadow, grove, and stream,
> The earth, and every common sight,
> To me did seem
> Apparelled in celestial light

Tragically, Wordsworth said, the child is socialized into an adult who loses this sensitivity. Wherever the person turns, "There hath past away a glory from the earth."

Ultimately, though, Wordsworth felt we need not despair. We can still recapture our childhood love for nature, at least to some extent.

Though nothing can bring back the hour

Of splendour in the grass, of glory in the flower;

    We will grieve not, rather find

    Strength in what remains behind;

    In the primal sympathy

    Which having been must ever be.

I don't know how we can determine if, as Wordsworth held, children actually see God's handiwork in nature. But it does seem that children experience nature and animals with wonder and delight.

Alcott

A mid-nineteenth-century educator who took Wordsworth very seriously was A. Bronson Alcott. Alcott believed children do, indeed, possess unique spiritual insight and adults should be alert to it.

Alcott is best-known as the father of Louisa May Alcott, the author of *Little Women*. He also was an influential member of the loose-knit group of Concord, Massachusetts, intellectuals that included Emerson, Thoreau, and Nathaniel Hawthorne.

Alcott, who was largely self-educated, was a dreamer. Lacking a mind for practical matters, he started many projects and failed at all of them. He first worked as a traveling peddler, but he couldn't make a living at it. He founded several schools that centered on children's natural ways of thinking, but all the schools closed within a few years. At Thoreau's suggestion, Alcott traveled to the West, hoping to earn money by giving philosophical lectures, but he returned home tired, hungry, and cold—with only a dollar in his pocket.

Alcott also helped establish a utopian community, a vegan agricultural adventure called Fruitlands. But he spent so much time singing the praises of the farm that he neglected the crops, and this project failed, too.

Despite all these defeats, Alcott's idealism inspired his Concord friends. It encouraged them to think outside conventional boundaries.

Alcott was so impressed by Wordsworth's view that children come directly from God that he tried to learn about spiritual matters from his pupils. Primarily, he hoped children could teach him through conversations about scripture. In the end, he didn't seem to gain any specific insights, but his effort stood out because he turned the usual teacher/student relationship on its head. Instead of trying to teach children, he tried to learn from them.

On a personal level, Alcott felt fortunate simply to have associated with children. From them he acquired faith and hope. And Alcott left future educators with thoughts to ponder. He said, for example, that teachers should approach children with humility because their minds, compared to ours, are often "on a larger scale . . . deeper, tenderer, and wider."

Since Alcott loved Wordsworth's poetry, it's surprising that he didn't pay more attention to children's feelings for nature. One person who did so was his friend Thoreau, whom we discussed in chapter 1. Thoreau shared Wordsworth's lament that we lose our exquisite sensitivity to nature as we grow up. Indeed, when Thoreau wrote most passionately about this loss, he sprinkled his thoughts with bits of Wordsworth's poetry.

Artists

For several decades, those who admired childlike perception were primarily art critics and painters. In Thoreau's day (in the mid-nineteenth century), the critic John Ruskin urged painters to perceive nature through "an innocence of the eye," as if seeing it for the first time. Ruskin's advice sparked painting's Impressionist movement. Impressionists like Claude Monet abandoned traditional studio techniques—like making "important" figures clearer than other ones. Instead, the Impressionists painted the world the way it immediately struck their senses.

Childlike perception was also prized during the early twentieth-century modern art movement. In1912, the Russian painter Wassily Kandinsky suggested that the artist, like the child, has a special ability to see "the inner harmony of things." Paul Klee sometimes actually imitated children's ways of painting in order to recapture the childhood spirit.

Dewey

In the field of education, one of the few prominent individuals to urge childlike attitudes was John Dewey. In his classic 1916 book *Democracy and Education*, Dewey suggested that the purpose of education is to promote intellectual growth. But Dewey added that growth doesn't always move from childhood to adulthood. Adult thinking may often be more advanced, but when it comes to intellectual traits such as "curiosity, unbiased responsiveness, and openness of mind, we may say the adult should be growing into childlikeness."

Innovative Psychologists

In the middle of the twentieth century, a few prominent psychologists tried to take their field in a new direction. Abraham Maslow and others were dissatisfied with behaviorism, which still dominated psychology. They believed that behaviorism's view of humans, as the product of external rewards and punishments, was much too narrow.

Many of the psychologists were also concerned about the pressures of social conformity, which limits people's creativity and openness to experience. Ernest Schachtel noted, for example, that when people take a trip they pay attention to the sites that "one simply must see." They do not perceive their surroundings in a fresh manner. Young children, Schachtel and Maslow said, aren't so hemmed in by cultural expectations. They see the world more openly, and their perception is richer. This is why great artists and others have tried to recapture the childhood outlook.

A similar point was made by Heinz Werner. Werner had created a sweeping theory of development in the 1920s, when he was in Hamburg, Germany. He came to the United States in the 1930s to escape Adolf Hitler and continued to refine his theory. Late in his life, he countered the common belief that the most valuable thinking is that of the rational adult. To the contrary, Werner said, the most creative individuals initially experience things in the manner of young children. That is, creative people at first pay attention to global impressions that are fused with emotions—what they sometimes call their gut-level impressions—before they engage in more intellectual analyses.

Maslow, Schachtel, and Werner echoed the views of Wordsworth and Thoreau. All believed adults should regain children's fresh and open experience. But Wordsworth and Thoreau said something more specific. In their view, it's not just that the child is more open to experience in general. Children's responsiveness is at its peak when they are in contact with *nature*. The mid-twentieth-century scholar who most notably advanced this Wordsworth/Thoreau theme was Edith Cobb.

Cobb

Edith Cobb didn't have an academic résumé. She was instead a kind of patron—a well-to-do woman who served on the boards of several organizations. She worked especially hard to support social work institutions and documentary films. As part of these activities, Cobb associated with some well-known intellectuals, including the anthropologist Margaret Mead, but Cobb seemed intimidated in their presence. Still, she read widely, taking a strong interest in child development, and became a social worker in order to learn about a variety of children firsthand.

Then, in 1959, Cobb published an article called "The Ecology of Imagination in Childhood," followed by a 1977 book with the same title. These works struck a chord with several researchers who were conducting pioneering studies on children's feelings about nature. These investigators, who included Roger Hart, Robin Moore, and David Sobel, felt that Cobb confirmed their own emerging insights. Sobel says he was so excited by Cobb's 1959 article that, "I got tingles up and down my spine." He showed Cobb's article to dozens of colleagues and friends, saying, "You've got to read this!"

Cobb's primary source of data was approximately three hundred autobiographical recollections of gifted individuals. She studied writings from many cultures, beginning in the sixteenth century. Cobb also observed contemporary children's play and artwork and drew on scientific writings.

From these sources, Cobb concluded that childhood holds the key to human creativity. Creative geniuses are those who maintain their childhood state of mind. They continue to be playful, full of wonder, and open to new discoveries. As an illustration, Cobb quoted Isaac Newton, who said that when he was making his discoveries,

> I seem to have been only like a boy playing on the seashore, and diverting myself in now and then finding a smoother pebble or a prettier shell than ordinary, while the great ocean of truth lay all undiscovered before me.

Cobb found that there is a special period, between the ages of six and twelve, when children are especially enchanted with nature—when, as she put it, they experience it "in some highly evocative way." During this time, Cobb added, children even experience themselves as part of the natural world. For example, Cobb quoted the art critic Bernard Berenson, who recalled a summer morning when he was five or six years old:

> A silver haze shimmered and trembled over the lime trees. The air was laden with their fragrance. The temperature was like a caress. I . . . climbed up a tree stump and felt suddenly immersed in Itness. I did not call it by that name. I had no need for words. It and I were one.

Cobb said gifted adults return in memory to vivid childhood experiences in order to renew their sense of wonder and creative power—a renewal, Cobb added, that would be good for everyone to try.

Cobb's work was important but short on specifics. She wrote in generalities, implying that her statements about gifted adults were true of every single one of them. Louise Chawla followed up with a more precise and detailed study of thirty-eight twentieth-century autobiographies.

Chawla found that the kinds of intense memories Cobb described weren't as universal as she suggested. In Chawla's study, fifteen of the thirty-eight writers described such memories. Nor were the memories confined to the ages six to twelve; some "treasured memories originated in early childhood and adolescence."

In addition, Chawla's autobiographies didn't always refer to childhood experiences as a source of adult creativity. The authors more frequently described how their childhood feelings of oneness with nature provided an inner calm that later helped them get through personal difficulties. They echoed Wordsworth, who felt that his childhood connection with nature provided him with lasting comfort—a "holy calm."

Although Chawla's findings differed from Cobb's in some respects, Chawla confirmed Cobb's impressions in a general way. Like Cobb, Chawla found that children's nature experiences can have a profound and positive effect on personal development.

The Concept of Neoteny

In her writings, Cobb discussed the biological concept of *neoteny*, which refers to a lengthy childhood. Cobb suggested that during the course of evolution our species developed a prolonged childhood because it strengthened our openness to experience—our ability to see the world in fresh and new ways. Our slow development gave this open outlook time to take a firm hold in the human personality.

A few years after Cobb published her book, the anthropologist Ashley Montagu described the concept of neoteny in more detail. In a highly readable book titled *Growing Young*, Montagu proposed that neoteny provides humans with a very large number of valuable traits, including curiosity, imagination, playfulness, open-mindedness, willingness to experiment, humor, energy, honesty, enthusiasm, and joy. Montagu suggested that although Western culture hasn't fully appreciated these traits, they have evolutionary value, helping us meet life's challenges.

A New Breed of Adult

Most of the writers I have covered have looked upon childhood as a time when we experience the world openly and freshly because the mainstream culture has yet to get its grip on us. These writers have urged us, as adults, to get outside our culture in order to renew our childhood mode of perception.

More recently the journalist and novelist Christopher Noxon has endorsed a different approach. Countless adults, Noxon says, have discovered that they can feel young and energetic by *participating* in the mass culture— at least that part geared to children and youth.

In his 2006 book, *Rejuvenile*, he enthusiastically describes this "new breed of adult":

Whether buying cars marketed to consumers half their age, dressing in baby-doll fashions, or bonding over games like Twister or stickball, this new band of grown-ups refuses to give up things they never stopped loving, or revels in things they were denied or never got around to as children.

Noxon observes that these new adults—the "rejuveniles"—frequently marry later in life, postpone childbirth, and live longer in their parents' homes. This does not mean, however, that they ignore adult responsibilities. They do have jobs, and some have children. But they embrace childhood amusements. They play in kickball leagues, go to Disney World, and celebrate birthdays at Chuck E. Cheese. They ride skateboards, play video games, and collect Star Wars cards. To the rejuveniles, Noxon says, the culture of children "brims with qualities—wonder, adventure, absurdity, make-believe—in short supply in the adult world."

Noxon said that many of the rejuveniles were Generation X, but many also were younger or older. In any case, the behavior patterns he described in 2006 didn't go away. In fact, in 2017 U.S. adults were marrying and having children even later than in 2006. They also were even more likely to live in their parents' homes. And, if video games are any indication, adults didn't give up young people's amusements. The gamer's average age was thirty-three in both 2005 and 2018. Similarly, Disney amusement parks continued to appeal to adults without children.

I am convinced that the rejuvenile lifestyle can be fun. But it is not the lifestyle I am advocating. A major theme of this book is that we need to get outside the conventional society and become more receptive to nature.

It is nature, not commercial amusements, that brings wonder, beauty, and comfort to our lives.

Today, the need to free ourselves from the strictures of mainstream culture has become especially urgent. Our commercial society has developed a variety of electronic screen devices—from TVs to smartphones and tablets—that keep people's attention fixed on the devices' screens. Even when people go to the beach or a park, they fixate on their devices. They do not experience birdsong, gentle breezes, or the play of sunlight on the water. They are oblivious to nature's sensations and the gifts of the spirit that can come with them.

Appendix B

. . . .

Some Remarkable
Strengths of Childhood

1. **Sense of wonder.** In the mid-twentieth century,
   Maslow, Schachtel, Carson, and others wrote about
   the child's sense of wonder. Cobb suggested that
   wonder often begins when babies discover their
   hands and take delight in contemplating them.
   Child scholar Jean Piaget's observations suggest
   that this occurs at about two months of age. Piaget
   noted how infants also gaze with rapt attention at
   other objects, such as toys hanging from a bassinet,
   at this age or even a few weeks earlier. Children's
   sense of wonder is very strong during the next sev-
   eral years, when the world is magical to them, and
   then gives way to a more realistic outlook at the age
   of seven or so.

2. **Bold exploration.** In 1975, Margaret Mahler
   and her coauthors Fred Pine and Anni Bergman
   described how toddlers become consumed with the
   thrill of locomotion and exploration. Between the
   ages of about twelve and eighteen months, toddlers
   energetically investigate everything around them.
   As they climb couches and chairs and explore their

outdoor surroundings, they are impervious to knocks and falls. They often become so absorbed in their explorations that they pay no attention to the presence or absence of caregivers.

After eighteen months or so, toddlers become warier. In new settings, they often check if caregivers are available if needed. But during the period of bold exploration, toddlers' physical courage is like that of the bravest mountain climber.

3. **Make-believe play.** At twelve or thirteen months, children begin pretend acts, such as feeding a doll, and in the next few years their make-believe play becomes quite elaborate. Dorothy and Jerome Singer note, for example, that when children pretend that they are pirates, their efforts to find costumes, make a boat, sail the sea, and go under water to search for treasure involve "integrated actions, multiple roles [and] imaginary objects." Many young children also have an imaginary companion, whose adventures take on a life of their own. The Singers have called the ages three to six "the high season of imaginative play." After this age, children's general orientation to the world becomes more realistic.

4. **Affinity to nature.** Carson, Maria Montessori, and others have suggested that children have an innate love of nature, what the biologist E. O. Wilson has called *biophilia*. In addition, the poet Percy B. Shelley observed that children, more strongly than adults, feel oneness with nature—a point that has been elaborated upon by modern scholars such as Cobb, Sobel, Chawla, and Hart.

It's my impression that children's fascination with nature begins at one year, when they are thrilled by the sight of dogs and other animals. It isn't clear when children's special affinity to nature might end, but it often seems to last until the onset of adolescence.

Natural settings have such a strong effect on children that they stimulate children's creativity. For example, most of the poems children compose have to do with nature, as do many of their paintings. Children's make-believe play also is particularly rich in natural settings. Nature stimulates their imaginations.

5. **Artistic activities.** Between the ages of about two and eight, children throw themselves into artistic activities. They love to sing, draw, dance, and make up poems. While all their efforts can be lovely, the quality of their drawing has been most carefully researched. Howard Gardner has described how, between the ages of about five and eight, children's drawings are breathtakingly fresh, lively, and beautifully balanced. Gardner has called these years a "golden period of artistic development" and has likened the children's drawings to those of modern masters.

6. **The grasp of syntax.** In 1925, the Russian writer Kornei Chukovsky pointed out that children have a remarkable capacity to sort out linguistic rules. In 1949, Montessori independently made the same observation. Their observations, however, had no impact on academic research. Then, in the late 1950s and the 1960s, Noam Chomsky clarified just how amazing the child's achievement is. Ordinary

children master highly complex syntactic rules—
rules for creating sentences—by the age of five or
six. And, Chomsky added, immigrant children
readily master the syntax of a second language as
well—without formal instruction, just from other
children. Meanwhile, adults struggle mightily with
the task. Some researchers believe that this special
capacity is genetically determined and lasts until the
age of seven or so, while others think it might con-
tinue until adolescence.

Notes

Epigraph

Einstein letter quoted in Dukas & Hoffmann, 1979, p. 82. (Originally written in 1947.)

Preface

Gardner, 1980: 1994, pp. 20–21.

Chawla, 1990.

On Werner and study of pediatricians: Crain, 2011, pp. 97–98 & 114–15.

Natural settings promote rich make-believe play and sense of calm: Crain & Crain, 2014.

Introduction: Invisible Children

Epigraph, Ellison, R, 1995. *Invisible Man*. New York: Vintage International. p. 3. (Originally published in 1952.)

Ignoring Childhood

Ariès, 1962. For critiques of Ariès, see Crain, 2011, pp. 4–5.

Transition to "future adult" image: Crain, 2011, pp. 5–6.

The Standards Movement

"Education in the Absence of Children." Kane, J. 1995, p. 58.

Kindergartens: Levin & Van Hoorn, 2016; Fowler, 2018.

Opt Out movement: Bakerman, 2018; Wilson, C., 2019. On parental concerns: Kirylo, 2015, Organ, 2016.

Ignoring Wonder

Plato cited in Erikson, J. M., 1988, p. 29.

Goethe cited in Watts, 1951, p. 151.

Wonder includes a sense of mystery: See Cobb, 1977, p. 28.

In 1954, Maslow identified wonder in highly creative people: Maslow, 1954, pp. 214–15.

Maslow's description of perception in creative people: Maslow, 1962, pp. 70–72.

"intently, absorbed, spellbound..." Maslow, 1966, p. 100.

Joan Erikson, 1988, p. 23.

Academics' Blind Spots

Maslow, 1954, p. 223; Schachtel, 1959.

For a teacher's perspective on seeing children, see Ayers, 1993, chapter 2.

Chapter 1. Henry David Thoreau

Epigraph: "I yearn for one of those old..." Thoreau, 1961, pp. 49–50.

Most people unhappy: Thoreau, 1981a, pp. 116–17; 1981b, pp. 358–60.

"The mass of men..." Thoreau, 1981a, p. 111.

Alcott quote: Harding, 1982, p. 459.

Thoreau wanted each individual to find his or her own way: Thoreau, 1981a, p. 158.

"A different drummer..." Thoreau, 1981a, p. 345.

Early Years

Thoreau's parents and childhood: Harding, 1982, pp. 8–9, 17–19; Walls, 2017, p. 45.

"I remember how glad I was..." Thoreau, 1978, p. 86.

Rich, "if not in money, in sunny hours..." Thoreau, 1981a, p. 247.

Encountering Grand Ideas

Thoreau's meetings with Orestes Brownson: Harding, 1982, pp. 45–46; Robinson, 2004, chapter 1; Walls, 2017, pp. 73–75.

Thoreau read Emerson's book, *Nature*, during Thoreau's senior year: Robinson, 2004, p. 15.

Emerson on a "Universal Being" that circulates through nature and us: Emerson, 2003a, p. 6.

Transcendentalism as formed by the ideas of Brownson and Emerson: Robinson, 2004, pp. 11–13.

Thoreau's commencement essay: Harding, 1982, p. 50.

Thoreau began friendship with Emerson: Robinson, 2004, p. 11; Harding, 1982, p. 61.

Emerson on conformity and self-reliance: Emerson, 2003b, pp. 63–65. Emerson on the spirit in us and nature: Emerson, 2003c, p. 133.

Emerson-led discussion groups: Harding,1982, pp. 63, 65.

Thoreau imitated Emerson's mannerisms: Walls, 2017, p. 90.

Emerson and Thoreau's on-again, off-again relationship: Walls, 2017, p. 87.

Occupations

First job after college as a teacher and disagreement over corporal punishment: Walls, 2017, pp. 85–86.

Thoreau and his brother at the Concord Academy: Harding, 1982, pp. 81–88; Walls, 2017, p. 97.

John died of lockjaw nine months later: Walls, 2017, p. 119; Harding, 1982, pp. 122, 134.

Walls suggests Thoreau came out of emotional crisis: Walls, 2017, p. 129

Thoreau's jobs. Surveying and other jobs: Harding, 1982, p. 186; Walls, 2017, p. 258. Pencil business: Harding, pp. 16–17. Odd jobs in Emerson home, Harding, pp. 127–28.

Walden Pond

Life at Walden Pond: Harding, 1982, pp. 179, 186. To get to the bare essence of life: Thoreau, 1981a, p. 172.

Sales of *Walden* in Thoreau's his lifetime: Harding, 1982, p. 340. A classic that sold millions: Witherell, 1995.

Visitors' descriptions of Thoreau: Harding, 1982, pp. 193, 173.

Socially awkward. Harding: 1982, pp. 67, 309; Walls, 2017, p. 304.

Relationship with Alcott: Thoreau, 1961, p. 111; Harding, 1982, pp. 66–68.

Rapport with children: Harding, 1982, p. 193.

Children brought him eggs: Harding, 1982, p. 406.

Thoreau introduced young people to his "family" of animals: Harding, 1982, p. 193.

"Thoreau was a boy at heart." Harding, 1982. p. 355.

Native Americans "stood nearer to wild nature than we." Thoreau, 1961, p. 193.

"As if [Native American] spirits willed him to be the inheritor..." Harding, 1982, p. 138.

The essence of nature is her wildness. Thoreau, 2010, p. 19.

Social institutions domesticate us. Thoreau, 1961, pp. 17, 31, 82, 83, 177.

"The captain of a huckleberry party." Walls, 2017, p. 308.

Not until after Thoreau's death did Emerson appreciate: Walls, 2017, p. 308.

Felt momentarily depressed because of a lack of social recognition: Thoreau, 1961, p. 172.

"Nature is always encouraging." Thoreau, 1961. p. 194.

A Sample of Thoreau's Humor

"I have now a library of nearly nine hundred volumes..." Thoreau, 1961, p. 254.

The poet had feathers: Harding, 1982, p. 305.

"It is not necessary that a man earn his living by the sweat..." Harding, 1982, p. 187.

"We are in great haste to construct a magnetic telegraph..." Thoreau, 1981a, p. 144.

"I did not know we had ever quarreled." Harding, 1982, p. 464.

Civil Disobedience

Thoreau's arrest and night in jail: Walls, 2017, pp. 208–9; Harding, 1982, pp. 199–2002; Thoreau, 1981c.

Staples's motive for arrest unclear: Harding, 1982, p. 202.

Lecture and essay on civil disobedience: Harding, 1982, pp. 199–207; Walls, 2017, p. 249; Thoreau, 1981c.

The impact of Thoreau's essay: Witherell, 1995.

Animal Welfare

Thoreau's view of vegetarianism: Thoreau, 1981a, pp. 260–70.

Shared his knowledge with scientists: Walls, 2017, p. 307.

Came to feel guilty about killing for specimens: Walls, 2017, p. 345; see also Thoreau, 1978, p.114.

Should I "shoot you if I wanted to study you?" Harding, 1982, p. 356.

Learn more about animals by observing them living freely: Thoreau, 1961, p. 214. Thoreau, 1978, p. 113.

Trees

When elm cut down, "The fathers of the town... were not there." Higgins, 2017, p. 143.

"Long stretches of surveying always left him grouchy..." Walls, 2017, p. 286.

Later Years

Gave ringing lectures in Brown's defense. Harding, 1982, p. 416.

Thoreau spoke out when no one else would: Walls, 2017, p.431.

Alcott three years earlier appointed superintendent: Walls, 2017, p. 461.

Alcott let classes out early for the funeral. Walls, 2017, p. 499.

"The country knows not yet..." Harding, 1982, p. 467.

Fresh and Childlike Observation

On children's delight in breezes, Thoreau, 1961, p. 47; in butterflies, 1961, p. 209; in flowers, 1961, p. 77; in berries, 1961, p. 93; cows, 1961, p. 23. (Thoreau thought children's senses were so superior to adults' that they could hear music in bells and in tin pots where adults cannot: Thoreau, 2016a, p. 85).

In conventional perception, nothing new. Thoreau, 1961, pp. 98, 148, 177.

Scientific nomenclature. Thoreau, 1999b, p. 95.

The child's discovery of fishes. Thoreau, 1999b, pp. 87–88.

As if experiencing nature's impressions for the first time. Thoreau, 1999b, p. 95.

Receive nature's impressions just as they come to us: Thoreau, 1999b, p. 95; 1961, p. 99.

Adult mental habits deeply engrained: Thoreau, 1961, p. 98.

We value our accumulated knowledge: Thoreau, 2010, p. 29.

"A sauntering of the eye." Thoreau, 1961, p. 99.

Goal is to be taken by surprise: Thoreau, 1961, pp. 210, 214.

Lilies suddenly unfolded: Thoreau, 1984, p. 115.

"I am struck by the splendid crimson-red..." Thoreau, 1962, p. 1039 (July 30, 1856 entry).

"Looking toward the sun..." Thoreau, 2016a, p. 235 (July 18, 1852 entry).

Walks at night: Robinson, 2004, pp. 140–47; Thoreau, 2019, p. 117; 1961, p. 98.

"On all sides..." Thoreau, 2019, p. 117.

"An aboriginal wildness in his strain." Thoreau, 1961, p. 87.

The flicker: Thoreau, 1961, p. 193.

The thrush "launches forth one strain..." Thoreau, 1961, p. 116.

It "is no opera music...there is the liquid coolness..." Thoreau, 2016a, p. 190 (July 5, 1852 entry).

"Wherever a man hears it..." Thoreau, 2016a, p. 190 (July 5, 1852 entry).

Such "divine, heavenly pleasure..." Thoreau, 1961, pp. 47–48.

On Ruskin: Richardson, 1986, p. 359.

Thoreau's disappointment in Ruskin: Thoreau, 1961, pp. 183, 188.

Thoreau learned a tremendous amount about nature: Walls, 2017, p. 439.

Thoreau worried his outlook was becoming hardened and narrow. Thoreau, 1961, p. 53.

"It's only when we forget our learning..." Thoreau, 1961, p. 210.

Combining the childhood and adult outlooks. Thoreau, 1999b, p. 92.

"The keen joy and discrimination of the child..." Thoreau, 1999b, p. 92.

Unhurried Living

We cannot be in a rush: Thoreau, 1999a, p. 49.

Thoreau shed himself of destinations: Thoreau, 1961, p. 49.

He wanted to be open to...the moment: Thoreau, 1999a, pp. 49, 50.

In this way, he could perceive things as they are: Thoreau, 1961, p. 210.

Thoreau observed and touched frogs: Harding, 1982, p. 403.

Recollections by Mr. Murray, the farmer, of Thoreau and little girl: Harding, 1982, p. 404.

"If a man walks in the woods for the love of them..." Thoreau, 1981b, p. 356.

At One with Nature

"An infinite and unaccountable friendliness..." Thoreau, 1981a, p. 203.

"Shall I not have intelligence with the earth?..." Thoreau, 1981a, p. 207.

All life-forms use the same genetic code: Campbell & Reese, 2005, pp. 313–14.

All life-forms code proteins with the same amino acids: Carlson, 1989, p. 236.

"The humblest fungus..." Thoreau, 1961, p. 200.

"There is a calmness of the lake..." Thoreau, 1961, p. 44.

"It is not merely crow calling to crow..." Thoreau, 1961, p. 140.

"Shall we not have sympathy with the muskrat..." Thoreau, 1961, p. 126.

Getting into the Seasons

Spring is the time to be cheerful like the birds: Thoreau, 1961, p. 52.

Summer is a time to relax: Thoreau, 1961, p. 89.

Autumn is for reflection, winter for solidifying...thoughts. Thoreau, 1961, p. 126.

Too much time indoors. Thoreau, 1961, pp. 83, 100.

We "are not well in them." Thoreau, 1961, p. 119.

"...how is it that light comes into the soul?" Thoreau, 1961, p. 48.

"...till one day the sun shall shine more brightly..." Thoreau, 2010, p. 36.

A Sample of Thoreau Quotes

"To perceive freshly..." Thoreau, 1961, p. 48.

"The child plucks its first flower..." Thoreau, 1961, p. 77.

"If you would be wise..." Thoreau, 1999b, p. 41.

"Take an original..." Thoreau, 1961, p. 95.

"Go not to the object..." Thoreau, 1961, p. 99

"Wisdom does not inspect..." Thoreau, 1999a, p. 60.

"Experience is in the fingers..." Thoreau, 1961, p. 31.

"It is only necessary to behold..." Thoreau, 1961, p. 148.

"All the phenomena of nature..." Thoreau, 2016a, p. 158.

"Bathe in all the tides of nature..." Thoreau, 1961, p. 119.

"I hear the universal cock-crowing..." Thoreau, 1961, p. 91.

"The sound of the crickets..." Thoreau, 2016a, p. 109.

"The wood thrush is a more modern..." Thoreau, 1961, p. 17.

"Nowadays almost all man's improvements..." Thoreau, 2010, p. 6.

On fishes whose migration is blocked... Thoreau, 2016b, p. 21.

"I love even to see the domestic animals..." Thoreau, 2010, p. 25.

"Where the most wonderful wild-flowers grow..." Thoreau, 2016a, p. 104.

"Here is this vast, savage, mother of ours..." Thoreau, 2010, p. 28.

"In society, in the best institutions..." Thoreau, 2010, p. 28.

"What does education do!..." Thoreau, 1999a, p. 39.

"I hate museums..." Thoreau, 1984, p. 77.

"How deep the ruts of tradition..." Thoreau, 1999a, p. 35.

"It is possible..." Thoreau, 1961, p. 50.

"Let your life be a counter friction..." Thoreau, 1981c, p. 92.

Chapter 2. Albert Einstein

Epigraph: Hoffmann, 1972, p. 248.

"The victorious child." Erikson 1982, p. 151.

"Succeeded in saving the child in himself." Erikson, 1982, p. 155.

The "education-machine." Einstein, 1959, p. 3.

Early Years

On Einstein's mother and father: White & Gribbin, 1994, p. 4.

Didn't speak during his first three years: Hoffmann, 1972, p. 14.

Paused before putting sentences into words: White & Gribbin, 1994, p. 5.

Pauses in speech lasted until he was seven years old: Erikson, 1982, p. 152.

Socially a rather isolated child: White & Gribbin, 1994, p. 5;Vallentin, 1954, p. 17.

"My father showed me a compass..." White & Gribbin, 1994, p. 9.

Experience in Catholic school: White & Gribbin,1994, p. 9.

Experience in Gymnasium, beginning at age ten: White & Gribbin, 1994, p. 11. Hoffmann, 1972, p. 19.

"Dull, mechanized method of teaching." Hoffmann, 1972, p. 25.

"Even as a child, Albert recoiled instinctively from coercion..." Hoffmann, 1972, p. 18.

Performed most poorly on subjects that involved words and verbal texts: Hoffmann, 1972, pp. 19–20.

A teacher of Greek burst out that Albert would never amount to anything: White & Gribbin, 1994, p. 11.

Eagerly Learning Outside School

Albert's uncle gave him math problems: Hoffmann, 1972, p. 20.

At the age of twelve he came upon book on Euclidean geometry: Einstein, 1959, p. 9.

Talmey introduced Albert to popular science books: White & Gribbin, 1994, pp. 12–13; Hoffmann, 1972, p. 24.

Religious Crisis

Early religious instruction: White & Gribbin, 1994, p. 14.

Popular science books shook his faith in religion and all authority: Hoffmann, 1972, p. 24.

"Out there was a huge world..." Einstein 1959, p. 5.

The Violin

Einstein's quotes on learning the violin: Hoffmann, 1972, p. 20.

Dropout and Failure

When Albert was fifteen, parents' move and his decision to drop out: White & Gribbin, 1994, pp. 31–32.

Albert renounced German citizenship and Jewish faith; toured Italy: White & Gribbin, 1994, pp. 32–34.

Albert failed Polytechnic entrance exam; attended Swiss school: White & Gribbin, 1994, pp. 35–36.

A Year at a Child-Centered School

"Learning is not worth a penny..." Pestalozzi, 1951, p. 33.

On Pestalozzi: Gutek, 1999, especially pp. 11, 87, 103–4; Miller, 1990, pp. 76–77.

"Nature gave him self-confidence..." Vallentin, 1954, p. 29.

First "thought experiment" at age 16: Hoffmann, 1972, p. 28; Einstein, 1959, p. 58.

The Polytechnic Institute

Einstein entered Polytechnic Institute, deciding to pursue a teaching degree: White & Gribbin, 1994, p. 37; Hoffmann, 1972, p. 28.

Absorbed in joyful work in physics labs, with Grossmann helping him pass exams: Hoffmann, 1972, p. 30; Isaacson, 2017, p. 36.

"This coercion..." Einstein, 1959, p. 17.

"It is, in fact, nothing short of a miracle..." Einstein, 1959, p. 17.

Job Search

"I wasn't in the good graces..." Hoffmann, 1972, p. 32.

The head told Einstein, "You're a clever fellow! But..." Hoffmann, 1972, p. 32.

Einstein tried a series of temporary teaching and tutoring jobs: Hoffmann, 1972, pp. 32, 34. White & Gribbin, 1994, p. 47.

In 1901, Einstein submitted a research paper as a PhD dissertation that was rejected: Hoffmann, 1972, pp. 34–35.

In 1902, he began work in patent office: Hoffmann, 1972, p. 35.

"The Olympia Academy"

On the "Olympia Academy." Hoffmann, 1972, pp. 37–38; Feuer, 1974, p. 47.

Letter to Solovine, "In your brief and active existence ..." Feuer, 1974, pp. 47–48.

Einstein referred to his observations of children: Solovine, 1934, p. xv.

Prized children's curiosity and originality: Vallentin, 1954, p. 36.

Married Mileva Marić in 1903: White & Gribbin, 1994, p. 71.

Didn't give full attention to family: Vallentin, 1954, p. 43; Einstein, 2015, p. xxii.

Mileva didn't say much in Olympia Academy meetings: Solovine, 1934, p. xix.

Michele Besso was a sounding board: Hoffmann, 1972, pp. 41–42.

The 1905 paper cited no physicists except for a note thanking Besso. Isaacson, 2017, p. 123.

"Year of Miracles." Calaprice et al., 2015, p. xvi.

Relativity

In Newtonain physics, there is a single fixed system for measuring events: Feuer, 1974, pp. 58–59; Hoffmann, 1972, pp. 61, 63.

Einstein observed that time measurement is relative, depending on whether observer at rest or in motion. Isaacson, 2017, pp. 123–24.

Impossible to travel the speed of light: Bodanis, 2000, pp. 49–53.

Kaku's metaphor: Kaku, 2004, pp. 59–60, 62.

Einstein was exhausted after first 1905 paper on relativity: Vallentin, 1954, p. 46.

Second special relativity paper in 1905 took steps toward famous $E = mc^2$ equation: Hoffmann, 1972, p. 81.

Einstein's sister said physicists paid little attention to Einstein's 1905 papers: Isaacson, 2017, pp. 140–41.

Planck encouraged physicists to pay attention: Hoffmann, 1972, p. 83; Isaacson, 2017, pp. 140–41.

GPS systems rely on concept of time dilation: Calaprice et al., 2015, p. 211.

Timeline 1901 to 1921

1905. Submits the second of the papers as PhD dissertation: Hoffmann, 1972, p. 55.

1906. Receives PhD: Calaprice et al., 2015, p. xvi.

1907. Publishes $E = mc^2$: Hoffmann, 1972, p. 81.

1907. Begins work on general relativity: Hoffmann, 1972, p. 84; Isaacson, 2017, p. 145.

1909. Assumes first full-time paid faculty position: Hoffmann, 1972, p. 88.

1915. Reports that general theory of relativity predicts orbit of Mercury: Isaacson, 2017, p. 218.

1915. Presents final general theory of relativity. Isaacson, 2017, p. 218.

1916. Publication of first full account of the general theory of relativity: Calaprice et al., 2015, p. 296. The work was titled *The Foundation of the General Theory of Relativity*.

1919. Dyson expeditions support general relativity: Hoffmann, 1972, pp. 29–133.

1921. Einstein awarded Nobel Prize: Hoffmann, 1972, p. 150.

The General Theory of Relativity

Einstein's work on general relativity received mathematical help from Grossmann: Hoffmann, 1972, pp. 116–17.

"Years of anxious searching in the dark..." Hoffmann, 1972, p. 124.

Curved space-time and metaphor of trampoline: Isaacson, 2017, p. 223.

Einstein told Hilbert about his work; didn't want to be scooped by Hilbert: Isaacson, 2017, pp. 212–16.

Einstein not motivated by social recognition but search for "sublimity and marvelous order" in nature: Einstein, 1982, p. 38. See also Einstein, 1982, p. 39.

Work comes "straight from the heart." Einstein, 1982, p. 227.

Einstein's work in November, 1915: Isaacson, 2017, pp. 214–20; Kaku, 2004, pp. 105–6.

"Majestic simplicity" and "indescribable beauty:" Hoffmann, 1972, pp. 120 &124.

Isaacson's conclusions on the Einstein-Hilbert priority debate: Isaacson, 2017, pp. 221–22.

Confirmation by Dyson expeditions made Einstein world famous: Hoffmann, 1972, p. 133.

Nobel Prize

Rejected nine times for Nobel Prize before receiving it in 1921: Calaprice et al., 2015, pp. 201–2.

Anti-Semitism played a role: Isaacson, 2017, p. 311.

In addition, many scientists remained skeptical of relativity: Calaprice et al., 2015, p. 202.

Nobel committee believed relativity was too theoretical: Isaacson, 2017, pp. 310–11, 313.

"God Does Not Play Dice"

"God does not play dice." Hoffmann, 1972, p. 193.

Attempts to develop a final unified field theory: Calaprice et al., 2015, pp. 224–26.

A Stranger in Public Society

Disheveled appearance: Vallentin, 1954, p. 27.

When Einstein tried to visit former teacher: White & Gribbin, 1994, pp. 11–12.

His mind probably drifted to scientific problems: Hoffmann, 1972, p. 249.

"Suddenly he would fall silent in social gatherings": Vallentin, 1954, p. 44.

For a detailed account of Einstein's two marriages, children, and friends, see Calaprice et al., 2015, pp. 51–80.

Einstein's wish to withdraw was increasing with age: Einstein, 2015, p. xxii.

Einstein recognized that his detachment came at an emotional cost: Einstein, 2015, p. xxii.

Vallentin observed a contradiction: Vallentin, 1954, p. 92.

Believed in world peace (Calaprice, 2011, pp. 248–49; Calaprice et al., 2015, pp. 260–61, 263–65), socialism (Calaprice, p. 298), freedom of thought (Calaprice, pp. 107, 298); formation of Israel (Calaprice et al., pp. 234–41), African American rights (Calaprice, pp. 311–13; Jerome & Taylor, 2006).

Einstein on vegetarianism: Calaprice 2011, pp. 453–54.

"Only a life lived for others…" Vallentin, 1954, p. 93.

"He loves their naivete…" Vallentin, 1954, p. 36.

The Power of Childhood

Results of autopsies: Calaprice et al., 2015, p. 127.

Erikson linked Einstein's creativity to his playfulness. Erikson, 1982, p. 155.

"I have no special gift..." Hoffmann, 1972, p. 7.

"There is such a thing as a passionate desire..." Vallentin, 1954, p. 30.

He joked that he kept asking himself questions children ask: Feuer, 1974, p. 63.

Amazing harmony of nature's laws: Einstein, 1982, p. 40.

"Everyone who is seriously involved..." Dukas & Hoffmann, 1979, p. 33.

Only catch glimpses: Dukas & Hoffmann, 1979, pp. 32, 39; Einstein, 2015, p. xxiii.

This sense of mystery is at the heart of religion, the arts, science—and childhood: White & Gribbin, 1994, p. 263.

"People like you and me..." Dukas & Hoffmann, 1979, p. 82.

Chapter 3. Charlotte Brontë

Epigraph. Song composed by Harry Dixon Loes in the 1920s.

Early Childhood

Date of family's move to Haworth: Harman, 2015, p. 23.

Descriptions of mother's personality and her ailment: Gaskell, 1997, pp. 37, 40.

Birthdates and birthplaces of children: Alexander & Smith, 2018, pp. xxxii–xxxiv.

Mother took to bed: Harman, 2015, p. 30.

Descriptions of father: Alexander & Smith, 2018, p. 98; Gaskell, 1997, pp. 34–35, 38, 41, 62. (It was also said that Mr. Brontë had an explosive temper, but he disputed this: Harman, 2015, p. 28.)

Aunt Branwell was generally distant: Gaskell, 1997, p. 49; Harman, 2015, p. 36.

The children were isolated from other children: Harman, 2015, p. 51.

"Hand-in-hand": Gaskell, 1997, p. 40.

Maria read others newspaper articles: Gaskell, 1997, p. 46.

Maria encouraged make-believe play: Harman, 2015, p. 37.

Children's instruction at home: Harman, 2015, p. 52.

Girls sent to a residential school that could prepare them for occupations open to women: Harman, 2015, p. 38.

A Miserable School

Instruction and conditions of the Cowan Bridge School: Harman, 2015, pp. 40, 42.

Deaths of the older sisters: Harman, 2015, p. 46.

Incredibly, Mr. Brontë sent Charlotte and Emily back to Cowan Bridge: Harman, 2015, pp. 47–48.

Heartbroken, and barely nine years old. Gaskell, 1997, pp. 60, 62, 70–71.

Description of Tabby: Harman, 2015, p. 50.

Home instruction for five years following Cowan Bridge: Harman, 2015, pp. 52, 78–79.

Drawing lessons: Alexander & Smith, 2018, p. xxxvi.

Children took charge of their own education: Gaskell, 1997, p. 50.

Exciting Books and Make-Believe Play

The books the children read from father's library: Harman, 2015, pp. 52–53.

Mr. Brontë brought toy soldiers to Branwell at night. Ratchford, 1949, p. 6.

"Emily and I jumped out of bed..." Gaskell, 1997, p. 67.

Charlotte's favorite figure was the Duke of Wellington: Harman, 2015, p. 59.

"Scandalous and ruthless...": Harman, 2015, p. 72.

Tiny script: Harman, 2015 pp. 54–56.

Children's artwork illustrated their stories and other fantasy productions: Harman, 2015, p. 80. Imaginary heroes were patrons of the arts. Alexander & Smith, 2018, p. 19.

"SIR,—It is well known..." Gaskell, 1997, p. 69.

Gaskell expresses concern for Charlotte's mental health: Gaskell, 1997, pp. 69–71.

Roe Head

"So short-sighted..."; a "little old woman." Gaskell, 1997, p. 78.

"So sick for home..." Gaskell, 1997, p. 78.

Charlotte stayed at Roe Head a year and a half: Alexander & Smith, 2018, p. 343.

Charlotte was too frail for sports, but had other engaging qualities: Gaskell, 1997, pp. 79–82.

Told stories to the girls: Harman, 2015, p. 68.

An Inner Light

Charlotte was sometimes described as plain: Gaskell, 1997, pp. 74, 80; Harman, 2015, pp. 82–83.

"The sense of not being attractive haunted Charlotte all her life": Harman, 2015, p. 83.

"Usual expression was of quiet..." Gaskell, 1997, p. 74.

"We wove a web in childhood" from the poem, "Retrospection" in C. Brontë, 1988, p. 3. (Written at age nineteen: Ratchford, 1949, p. 110.)

Back Home from Roe Head

At Roe Head, Charlotte made two lifelong friends: Gaskell, 1997, p. 91; Harman, 2015, pp. 60–62.

Charlotte returned home at age sixteen to teach sisters: Harman, 2015, p. 71.

"Every moss..." Harman, 2015, p. 71.

"Passing amid the deepest shade..." Harman, 2015, p. 72.

Teaching at Roe Head

At nineteen, Brontë was invited back to Roe Head as a teacher: Harman, 2015, p. 87.

"Nobody knew what ailed her but me..." Gaskell, 1997, p. 104.

"I felt in my heart..." Gaskell, 1997, p. 104.

"Fat-headed oafs." Ratchford, 1949, p. 110.

"Must I from day to day sit..." Ratchford, 1949, p. 110.

Brontë tried to maintain a professional demeanor: Harman, 2015, p. 92.

Sometimes she became so lost in her fantasies: Ratchford, 1949, pp. 111–12.

Risk of madness: Harman, 2015, pp. 99, 102.

"If you knew my thoughts..." Harman, 2015, p. 97.

Letter to Southey and his reply: Harman, 2015, pp. 100–3.

Brontë "would turn sick and trembling..." at damp new school: Gaskell, 1997, p. 125.

Brontë returned home and recovered: Harman, 2015, pp. 108–9.

Governess

"Spiritual communion, yes; love..." Harman, 2015, p. 87.

Brontë's quotes on work as governess: Harman, 2015, p. 116.

"faculties unexercised." Harman, 2015, p. 135.

Farewell to Angria

Abandoned Angrian writings at twenty-three: Ratchford, 1949, pp. 148–49.

Attempted to establish own school: Harman, 2015, pp. 183–84. No pupils applied. Ratchford, 1949, p. 161.

In Brussels, fell in love with married teacher who didn't reciprocate: Ratchford, 1949, pp. 164–65.

"One day resembles another..." Gaskell, 1997, p. 207.

A Magnificent Discovery

"...stirred my heart..." Harman, 2015, pp. 207–8.

"To Imagination." Bronte, E., 2014.

Book of poems under pseudonyms. Harman, 2015, p. 210.

The sisters' books, *The Professor, Jane Eyre, Agnes Grey*, and *Wuthering Heights*. Harman, 2015, pp. 226–40.

Some of Charlotte's earlier, fantasy material appeared in her published poems and novels: Harman, 2015, pp. 208, 210–11; Ratchford, 1949, p. 150. (Emily and Anne also transferred poetry from their earlier, Gondal writings, to later works: Ratchford, 1949, pp. 136–69, 251–64).

"...the cooler clime of England." Ratchford, 1949, p. 150.

Losses and Loneliness

Deaths of Branwell, Emily, and Anne: Alexander & Smith, 2018, p. xiv.

"One by one I have watched them fall..." Harman, 2015, p. 271.

"Solitude..." "To sit in a lonely room." Gaskell, 1997, p. 297.

Discovery that Currer Bell was Charlotte. Gaskell, 1997, p. 306.

Life in London society. Harman, 2015, pp. 294–96; Gaskell, 1997, pp. 309, 312.

"When I felt such craving for support..." Gaskell, 1997, p. 382.

Visits and letters brought some relief. Gaskell, 1997, p 372.

Nature's beauty continued to stir and comfort: Gaskell, 1997, pp. 334–35, 343.

Shirley "was composed in the eager, restless..." Gaskell, 1997, p. 339.

"The faculty of imagination lifted me...": Gaskell, 1997, pp. 302–3.

Local shopkeeper's recollection. Gaskell, 1997, p. 216.

Brontë turned down three marriage proposals. Gaskell, 1997, p. 355.

Brontë enjoyed marriage. Harman, 2015, p. 340; Gaskell, 1997, p. 422.

Harman identifies the illness during pregnancy as hyperemesis gravidarum: Harman, 2015, p. 346.

Challenging Conventions

"No women that ever lived—ever wrote such poetry before." Harman, 2015, p. 208.

"Girls are protected..." Gaskell, 1997, p. 219.

"I speculate..." Gaskell, 1997, p. 220.

Jane Eyre

"I will prove you wrong..." Gaskell, 1997, p. 235.

Jane Eyre was the first novel to use a first-person child narrator. Harman, 2015 p. 48.

"And the Psalms..." Brontë, 2011, p. 32.

"No sir." Brontë, 2011, p. 32.

"Psalms are not interesting." Brontë, 2011, p. 33.

Jane's aunt takes Jane's "insolence:" Brontë, 2011, p. 33.

"*Speak* I must..." Brontë, 2011, p. 36.

"Ere I finished this reply..." Brontë, 2011, p. 36.

Harman says "the first readers of *Jane Eyre*..." Harman, 2015, p. 48.

"Dispatches from a new frontier." Harman, 2015, p. 49.

"Mind's eye dwell..." Brontë, 2011, p. 111.

"Nobody knows how many rebellions..." Brontë, 2011, pp. 111–12.

Chapter 4. Howard Thurman

Epigraph: Thurman, 1998, p. 128.

Trip to Ceylon, Burma, & India: Thurman, 1979, p. 103.

Lectures introduced Gandhi to U.S. civil rights movement: Williams & Dixie, 2003, p. 200; Smith, 2007, p. 140.

Questions about Thurman as a representative of Christianity: Thurman, 1979, pp. 113–14, 118, 125, 135.

"The Christian movement has been on the side of the strong..." Thurman, 1996, p. 20.

Thurman's views were rooted in his mystical experiences of the unity of life: Tumber & Fluker, 1998, p. 11.

Beginnings

Family background and childhood: Thurman, 1979, pp. 4–13.

"Oh Howard, that didn't hurt you..." Thurman, 1979, p. 12.

"You are not slaves!..." Thurman, 1979, p. 21.

Nature

"The night..." Thurman, 1979, pp. 7–8.

"I needed the strength of that tree..." Thurman, 1979, pp. 8–9.

"I could reach down in the quiet places..." Thurman, 1979, p. 9.

"I had the sense that all things..." Thurman, 1979, pp. 225–26.

"...a certain overriding immunity..." Thurman, 1979, p. 8.

Schooling

Early schooling and incident at the train station: Thurman, 1979, pp. 24–25.

Won literary prizes and was valedictorian: Tumber & Fluker, 1998, p. 3.

John Hope's manner of addressing students at Morehouse College: Thurman, 1979, p. 36.

Decision to become a minister: Thurman, 1979, p. 45.

Developing a Philosophy

Time at Rochester Theological Seminary: Thurman, 1979, pp. 46–47, 52; Tumber & Fluker, 1998, p. 4.

"...wonderland of the spirit..." Thurman, 1979, p. 225.

"...an instinctual sense of the unity of all life." Thurman, 1979, p. 225.

On Schreiner being white: Thurman, 1979, p. 225.

Marriage to Kate Kelley and pastorate in Oberlin: Thurman, 1979, p. 65.

Named daughter after Olive Schreiner: Thurman, 1979, p. 75.

Purchased a book for ten cents by Rufus Jones and goes to Haverford College: Thurman, 1979, pp. 74, 76–77; Smith, 2007, pp. 33–38.

Joining mysticism with social action: Thurman, 1998, pp. 116–17; Smith, 2007, pp. 35–38.

Tragedy and Ocean Voyages

Faculty a Morehouse and Spelman Colleges: Thurman, 1979, p. 78.

Wife's death and decision to make ocean voyage to Europe: Thurman, 1979, p. 82.

"There were times..." and "like a homecoming of the spirit." Thurman, 1979, p. 249.

Marriage to Sue Bailey and new faculty position at Howard: Thurman, 1979, pp. 84–86.

Reservations about trip to Burman, Ceylon, and India: Thurman, 1979, pp. 103–4.

The sea raged: Thurman, 1979, p. 109.

"The whole sweep..." and "undifferentiated..." Thurman, 1979, pp. 109–10.

Discussions with Asian hosts on Christianity: Thurman, 1979, pp. 113–36.

A Message of Love

"If a Roman soldier..." Thurman, 1996, p. 23.

"...all the cast-down..." Thurman, 1996, p. 18.

Many feel they must be prepared to protect their lives: Thurman, 1996, p. 24.

Hatred gives a sense of righteous indignation: Thurman, 1996, p. 72.

Hatred soon gets out of control: Thurman, 1996, pp. 76–77.

"Hatred is destructive to hated and hater alike." Thurman, 1996, p. 25.

Not to love our enemies' actions, but as fellow humans: Thurman, 1996, p. 84.

"...see the individual white man in the context..." Thurman, 1996, p. 90.

Debbs quote: Thurman, 1998, p. 128.

"no age, no race..." Thurman, 1996, pp. 98–99.

"simple heart": Thurman, 1996, p. 85.

Pastoral Leader

Initially blocked from visiting parishioner in hospital: Thurman, 1979, p. 154.

Provided spiritual counseling to numerous activists, including King: Tumber & Fluker, 1998, p. 6.

"was able to dig deep into..." Tumber & Fluker, 1998, p. 13.

The pastoral leader of the civil rights movement: Tumber & Fluker, 1998, p. 13.

King carried *Jesus and the Disinherited*: Tumber & Fluker, 1998, p. 131.

Meditations of the Heart

We yearn for "some haven, some place of retreat..." Thurman, 1981, p. 46.

The recommended meditation process: Thurman, 1981, pp. 20, 27–29.

In meditation we gain peace and strength from being rooted in something greater. Thurman, 1981, pp. 20, 137–40.

Alternatives to defining this presence as God: Crain, 2014, p. 55.

"All life is one." Thurman, 1979, p. 269.

Concluding Thoughts

"...all things...were one lung..." Thurman, 1979, pp. 225–26.

"Embraced" and "held secure." Thurman, 1979, p. 7. Strength of tree and "rooted..." p. 8

Extended Discussion on the Unity of Life

"...particularly human life." Thurman, 1998, p. 116.

For other examples of Thurman's focus on *human* life, see Thurman, 1981, pp. 115, 117–18; 1998, pp. 116, 164.

Nature is too perfect. Thurman, 1998, pp. 87–89.

But later saw nature in disarray. Thurman, 1998, p. 276.

We do not appreciate Native American wisdom and we feel rootless: Thurman, 1998, p. 276.

Chapter 5. Jane Goodall

Epigraph: Goodall, 2003.

Mr. H.: Peterson, 2006, p. 45.

Early Years

Early life: Peterson, 2006, pp. 10–18; Goodall, 2003, p. 3; Goldberg, 1999.

"Jane, if you keep them here they'll die..." Goodall, 2003, p. 5.

"She did not scold me..." Goodall, 2003, pp. 6–7.

Parents divorced: Goodall, 2003, p. 17.

Not keen on school: Goodall, 2003, p. 11: Peterson, 2006, p. 44.

"There, high above the ground..." Goodall, 2003, p. 20.

Thoughts in her tree: Goodall, 2003, p. 21.

"I think I went through all the Tarzan books..." Peterson, 2006, p. 46.

Continued reading Tarzan and Dr. Dolittle books at age seventeen: Peterson, 2006, p. 46.

Crush on new minister: Goodall, 2003, pp. 21–29.

Poem, "The lovely dunes..." Goodall, 2003, p. 30.

Secretarial school: Goodall, 2003, pp. 30–32.

Africa

Invitation to visit Africa: Goodall, 2003, p. 35.

"Limitless world of water..." Goodall, 2003, p. 39.

Meeting with Leakey: Goodall, 2003, p. 44; Peterson, 2006, p. 101.

Goodall learned a great deal working at museum: Goodall, 2003, p. 45.

"Slaughter of the innocents." Goodall, 2003, p. 54.

Goodall on dig with Leakeys and his discovery. Goodall, 2003, p. 46.

"I must find a way to watch..." Goodall, 1996, p. 46.

Leakey's plan to study chimpanzees: Peterson, 2006, p. 119.

"When he put it like that..." Goodall, 2003, p. 55.

A four-month study: Peterson, 2006, p. 204. Goodall, 2000, p. 7, says it was a six-month study.

Gombe Reserve only twenty square miles: Goodall, 1986, p. 45. Very hilly: Peterson, 2006, p. 182.

First Studies in Gombe

British government demanded a chaperone: Jane Goodall Institute U.K., 2020.

Early observations of chimps with aids and mother at base camp: Peterson, 2006, pp. 183–84, 187, 189, 194–97, 208; Goodall, 2003, p. 65.

Earlier field researchers hid behind blinds: Peterson, 2006, p. 215.

First observations of David Greybeard: Peterson, 2006, pp. 194, 198, 209.

George Schaller's visit: Peterson, 2006, p. 205.

Discovery of meat-eating: Peterson, 2006, p. 207.

Discovery of toolmaking: Peterson, 2006, pp. 207, 209; Goodall, 2003, pp. 66–67.

"Challenged human uniqueness." Goodall, 2003, p. 67.

Discoveries led to a National Geographic grant to extend research: Goodall, 2003, p. 67.

Explored without assistants or chaperone: Goodall, 2003, pp. 68–73; Peterson, 2006, pp. 232–33.

Like a Child in a Magical Forest

"...pressure was off." Goodall, 2003, p. 71.

Fascinated by whatever she encountered: Goodall, 2003, pp. 71–73.

"Everything is fresh..." and experiencing without words: Goodall, 2003, p. 79.

"...became intensely aware of the being-ness of trees..." Goodall, 2003, p. 73.

"...reached into the inner core..." Goodall, 2003, p. 78.

Peace of the forest within her: Peterson, 2006, p. 268.

"Good morning, Peak..." Goodall, 2003, p. 72.

David Greybeard was calm and gentle: Goodall, 2000, pp. 69, 268.

Goliath was athletic, aggressive, and brave: Goodall, 2000, pp. 73–74.

Flo was "tough as nails": Goodall, 2000, p. 80. Inexplicably attractive to male chimps: Peterson, 2006, p. 325.

Others were clever (Goodall, 2000, pp. 96–97), mischievous (Goldberg, 1999), shy (Goodall, 1986, p. 67), clownish (Goodall, 2000, p. 78), nurturing (Goodall, 2003, p. 89).

For mixtures of traits, see Goldberg, 1999, and Goodall, 1986, chapter 4.

Chimpanzees could reflect and plan: Goodall, 2003, pp. 75–76.

Chimpanzees showed emotions including joy (Goodall, 2000, p. 243), depression (Goodall, 1986, p. 67, Peterson, 2006, p. 215), aggression (Goodall, 1986, p. 122), love (Goodall, 2003, pp. 76–77), grief (Goodall, 2000, p. 216), curiosity (Peterson, 2006, p. 194), and awe (Goodall, 2003, p. 189).

They, too, kiss, hold hands . . . Goodall, 2003, p. 76.

Cambridge University

Leakey convinced Cambridge to admit Goodall into PhD program: Peterson, 2006, pp. 212–13.

Ethology: Peterson, 2006, pp. 270, 277; Crain, 2011, p. 40.

Cambridge ethologists' criticisms: Goodall, 2003, pp. 74–75; Peterson, 2006, p. 277.

David Greybeard

David Greybeard was first to tolerate close approach: Goodall, 2000, p. 267.

Chimps' visits to camp: Goodall, 2000, pp. 65–67, 80; 1986, p. 51.

Chimps' visit to camp enabled close observation: Goodall, 1986, p. 51; 2000, p. 145; Peterson, 2006, pp. 324, 353.

Goodall acknowledged she wasn't studying chimps in the wild: Goodall, 2000, pp. 80, 145.

Episode of David Greybeard and the nut: Goodall, 2003, p. 81; Peterson, 2006, p. 336.

"I needed no words . . ." and a language "far more ancient than words." Goodall, 2003, p. 81.

"The most significant of my life." Peterson, 2006, p. 336.

Cultural Traditions

Differences in tool use, Gombe vs. Bossou, Guinea: Goodall, 1986, pp. 537, 560.

Differences in grooming: Goodall, 1986, p. 144.

Differences in tool use and grooming can be regarded as cultural traditions: Goodall, 1986, p. 561.

Love and Disillusionment

Joined by wildlife photographer Hugo van Lawick: Peterson, 2006, p. 299.

Married in 1964; had son, Grub, two years later: Jane Goodall Institute, U.K., 2020; Peterson, 2006, p. 424.

Stopped following chimps to care for Grub: Goodall, 2003, pp. 86–87.

Goodall and van Lawick grew emotionally distant; one reason was religious differences: Peterson, 2006, p. 494.

God as a spiritual power Goodall felt all around her: Goodall, 2003, pp. 72, 93.

"This seemed a cruel ... offense ..." Peterson, 2006, p. 494.

Goodall's meeting and relationship with Derek Bryceson: Peterson, 2006, pp. 506, 518, 527, 534.

A heroic figure: Goldberg, 1999.

"Great inner turmoil": Peterson, 2006, p. 534.

Chimpanzee Violence

Chimpanzee violence: Goodall, 2003, pp. 111–12, 116; Goodall, 1986, pp. 504–5.

The violence shook Goodall's belief in a benevolent God: Goodall, 2003, p. 117; Goldberg, 1999.

The music "seemed to enter and possess my whole self..." Goodall, 2003, p. xiii.

There must be a God: Goodall, 2003, pp. xiii–xiv.

"A divine purpose ... " Goodall, 2003, p. 2.

Further Tragedies

Ten chimpanzee deaths in all: Goodall, 1986, p. 504.

Bryceson diagnosed with cancer and died: Peterson, 2006, pp. 578, 580.

His last weeks were worst of Goodall's life: Goodall, 2003, p. 157.

Rejected God: Goodall, 2003, p. 160.

Healing in Nature

Followed chimps when rainstorm hit: Goodall, 2003, p. 171.

"Lost in awe..." Goodall, 2003, p. 173.

"Even the mystics..." Goodall, 2003, p. 173.

"I truly believe it was a mystical experience." Goodall, 2003, p. 174.

Relative to science, Goodall placed a higher value on window of mystics: Goodall, 2003, p. 175; Goldberg, 1999.

Extended Discussion: Questioning Goodall's View of Chimpanzee Violence

Whereas Goodall saw chimpanzee aggression as innate propensity: Goodall, 1986, pp. 313, 531.

A chimp could eat fifty bananas at a sitting, and baboons fought with chimps over bananas: Goodall, 2000, p. 89.

Hoarding and quarrels arose among chimps: Power, 1991, p. 28; Goodall, 2000, pp. 140–41; 1986, pp. 51–52; Peterson, 2006, p. 345.

Tried banana boxes: Peterson, 2006, p. 353.

Power argues that frustration over closed boxes led to the lethal fighting: Power, 1991, pp. 28–29, 66–74.

Goodall grants that critics of banana feeding have a point (Goodall, 2003, p. 116), but sees violence as part of chimpanzees' natural territorial behavior (Goodall, 2003, pp. 127–28).

Power's view of normal chimpanzee group behavior and consequences of banana boxes: Power, 1991, pp. 60–73, 241–43.

Stanford, 2018.

A New Direction

"For twenty-five years..." Goodall, 2003, pp. 207–8.

Has become vegetarian: Goodall, 2003, pp. 221–22.

Until the COVID-19 pandemic, Goodall traveled 300 days a year: Wu, 2020.

Jo Jo had lived ten years "of utter boredom..." Goodall, 2003, p. 216.

"Only a sort of gratitude..." Goodall, 2003, p. 216.

"Jo Jo had committed no crime..." Goodall, 2003, pp. 216–17.

Conclusion

Piaget and Werner on self-world boundaries: Crain, 2003, pp. 97–102.

Children fall into mystical states: Cobb, 1977, pp. 32–34; Sobel, 2008.

"...part of a great unifying power." Goodall, 2003, p. 30.

"...with the spirit power of life itself." Goodall, 2003, p. 173.

Chapter 6. Rachel Carson

Epigraph: Carson, 1998a, p. 54.

Carson wanted to promote an appreciation of nature's wonder: Brooks, 1989, pp. 13, 323.

Childhood and Education

Carson's birth, childhood, and high school education: Lear, 1997, chapter 1.

The ocean held her greatest interest: Carson, 1998b, pp. 54, 77.

Carson quoted Dickinson: Carson, 1998b, pp. 148.

Carson's college experiences: Lear, 1997, pp. 39, 44; Brooks, 1989, p. 111.

"Felt united with an ancient time..." Lear, 1997, p. 62.

"My first impressions of the sea were sensory..." Carson, 1998b, p. 77.

MA thesis: Lear, 1997, p. 74.

Early Career

Began work for U.S. Bureau of Fisheries: Lear, 1997, p. 82.

Boss rejected "The World of Waters" pamphlet: Lear, 1997, p. 81.

Adopted Marian's two daughters: Lear, 1997, p. 84.

Becoming a Prominent Writer

Publication of "Undersea": Lear, 1997, pp. 87–88.

"... into a universe of all-pervading water." Brooks, 1989, p. 22.

"Thus, individual elements are lost to view..." Lear, 1997, p. 86.

The Sea Around Us was a best seller: Zwinger, 1991, xxvi.

"We are not so impatient that our own problems..." Carson, 1998b, p. 163; see also Carson, 1998b, pp. 88–89.

Carson as a public speaker: Lear, 1998, p. 76; Zwinger, 1991, p. xxiv; Lear, 1997, p. 260.

A Maine Cottage

Purchase of Maine cottage: Brooks, 1989, p. 129.

"The world was full of salt smell..." Brooks, 1989, p. 159.

"... creatures so exquisitely fashioned..." Brooks, 1989, p. 168.

"... gems, clear as crystal..." Carson, 1998b, p. 122.

Sand fragments were the end product of an ancient process: Carson 1998a, p. 122. Traveled largely with rains and rivers: Carson, 1998c, p. 126.

Carson and Dorothy Freeman fell in love: Lear, 1997, Ch. 11.

Exploring nature with young Roger: Brooks, 1989, p. 159.

New Challenges

In 1957, Carson had two projects in mind: Brooks, 1989, p. 205; Lear, 1998, p. 246.

Turning the Wonder Essay into a book "would be Heaven." Moore, 2008, p. 268.

Adoption and care for Roger: Brooks, 1989, p. 213.

A decade earlier [in 1945] Carson wrote *Reader's Digest* about pesticides, but no response: Lear, 1997, p. 312.

In 1957, new cases of toxic spraying caught her attention: Lear, 1997, pp. 312–13.

Huckins's letter. Brooks, 1989. p. 232.

Magazine editors called Carson an alarmist: Brooks, 1989, p. 237.

Mother's death: Brooks, 1989, p. 242.

Breast cancer. Brooks, 1989, p. 265.

Explanation of *Silent Spring* title: Carson, 2002, p. 103.

Radiation: Carson, 2002, pp. 6–7.

"Sprays, dusts, and aerosols..." Carson, 2002, pp. 7–8.

Silent Spring initiated modern environmental movement: Lear, 1998, p. x.

Brookses adopt Roger: Lear, 1997, p. 481.

Glimpses into Our Evolutionary Past

Ocean is the "mother of all life." Carson, 1991, p. 3.

Perhaps people recognize their far-off ancestry: Carson, 1991, p. 14.

"... carries in our veins a salty stream..." Carson, 1991, pp. 13–14.

Horseshoe crabs: Carson, 1998b, pp. 116–17.

Movements of the earth's outer crust: Carson, 1991, pp. 12–13.

Silurian Period: Johnson, 2020.

Whales: Carson, 1991, p. 45.

Humans' recent evolution: Carson, 1998b, pp. 87–88, 120, 160.

Scientists couldn't see human dependency on the environment: Carson, 1998b, pp. 167, 229, 244.

Emotional Responses

"If there is poetry in my book about the sea..." Brooks, 1989, p. 128.

Carson wanted scientists to look for nature's beauty: Brooks, 1989, p. 128.

"...heritage as a living creature." Carson, 1998b, p. 163.

Evolution is filled with mystery: Carson, 1998b, p. 194.

Universe will always be somewhat mysterious: Carson, 1998b, pp. 80, 96.

"...uneasy communication...that lies just beyond our grasp." Brooks, 1989, p. 329.

Three Unsolved Mysteries

Mystery of how life began: Carson, 1998b, p. 160; 1991, pp. 9–11. Still unknown, Marshall, 2016; Kaplan, 2021.

Mystery of oceans' depths: Carson, 1998b, pp. 80–82. Mysterious today, Ocean Explorer, 2017.

Migration of eels: Carson, 1998b, p. 19; Shanker, 2016. Of birds: Brink, 2020.

"...of strange, wild waters..." Carson, 1998b, p. 19.

Nature's Beauty and Mystery Keep Us Going

Nature's beauty brings "peace and spiritual refreshment." Carson, 1998b, p. 173.

Rock Creek Park: Carson, 1998b, p. 161.

"...untouched oases of natural beauty..." Carson, 1998b, p. 173.

"There is something infinitely healing..." Carson, 1998a, p. 89.

"...never bored..." Carson, 1998b, p. 159. Never "weary of life." Carson, 1998a, p. 88.

Nurturing Wonder—In Children and Ourselves

"...true instinct for what is beautiful..." Carson, 1998a, p. 54.

"...companionship of at least one adult..." Carson, 1998a, p. 55.

Children isolated from nature: Carson, 1998b, pp. 94, 161.

Cluttered parks: Carson, 1998b, pp. 94–162.

Beaches are rarely "wild and unspoiled." Carson, 1998b, p. 123.

"How can I possibly teach my child about nature?" Carson, 1998a, p. 55.

"...to know as to feel." Carson, 1998a, p. 56.

"What if I had never seen this before?" Carson, 1998a, p. 67.

We "can still drink in the beauty..." Carson, 1998a, p. 69.

"...fairy bell-ringer..." "I'm not sure I want to [see it]..." Carson, 1998a, p. 79.

Roger picked up names "without my knowing quite how..." Carson, 1998a, p. 30.

Science education. Carson, 1998b, pp. 165–66, 194.

"Some of the most gifted...biologists..." Carson, 1998b, pp. 165–66.

Darwin loved nature as a child: Darwin, 1958, pp. 44–45, 62.

Lorenz loved nature as a child: Crain, 2011, p. 40.

Goodall loved nature as a child: See chapter 5 of this book.

Nirenberg loved nature as a child: U.S. National Library of Medicine. n.d.

Concluding Thoughts

Damage humans have inflicted on the earth: Carson, 1998b, p. 163.

No remedy for "this unhappy trend": Carson, 1998b, p. 163.

Have less taste for destruction: Carson, 1998b, pp. 94, 163.

Woman's letter asking for vacation advice: Carson, 1998a, p. 90.

Chapter 7. Conclusion

Fresh Senses

"To perceive freshly..." Thoreau, 1961, p. 48.

On Husserl and phenomenology: Ellenberger, 1958, pp. 95–96; Overgaard, 2004.

"... to the things themselves": Overgaard, 2004.

Maslow and Schachtel: Crain, 2011, pp. 377–8, 383, and ch. 15.

Curiosity, Wonder, Mystery & Beauty

"... true instinct for what is beautiful..." Carson, 1998a, p. 54.

Play

"The faculty of imagination lifted me..." Gaskell, 1997, pp. 302–3.

"Play burst forth...": Eisen, 1990, p. 66.

For more on the role of imaginative playfulness in creative adults, see Bateson, 2015, Gardner, 1982, p. 253, and Gardner, 1994, pp. 20–21, 163–66.

Unity of Life

James, 2020, pp. 355–62.

Sobel, 2008. Sobel cites collections of mystical experiences by Hoffman, 1992, and Robinson, 1983.

Chawla, 1986.

All life-forms use the same genetic code: Campbell & Reese, 2005, pp. 313–14.

All life-forms code proteins with the same amino acids: Carlson, 1966, p. 236.

Genome research has revealed striking similarities across species. For example, humans share almost 99 percent of their DNA with chimpanzees. Chimpanzee Sequencing and

Analysis Consortium, 2005, Sept. 1. Humans even share about 30 percent of genes with yeast. Smith, 2005, p. 57.

PART II EPIGRAPH
Browning, 2015, pp. 82–83.

Chapter 8. Perceiving Nature with Fresh Senses

Ask Rachel Carson's Question
Carson, 1981, p. 67.

Walk off the Beaten Path
Thoreau on well-traveled roads: Loewer, 2009, p. 78.

Thoreau's discovery of beautiful weeds: Loewer, 2009, p. 191.

Night walk. See page 140 of this book.

Write Poetry
Snyder, 1992, p. 308.

Chapter 9. Recovering Play
Epigraph: Gibran, 2019, p. 42.

Brown says hectic lives: Brown, 2010, pp. 112, 124.

"The mass of men . . ." Thoreau, 1982, p. 111.

Brown defines play: Brown, 2010, p. 17.

Lose self-consciousness: Brown, 2010, p. 60.

Our society trivializes play: Brown, 2010, p. 144.

When we play we are happy and creative: Brown, 2010, pp. 59, 134.

What gave "unfettered pleasure"? Brown, 2010, p. 152. Was it drawing? Sewing? . . .: Brown, 2010, p. 207.

Take vacations: Brown, 2010, p. 127.

Play in relationships: Brown, 2010, pp. 161–71.

Joke around at work: Brown, 2010, p. 126. Playful attitude at work and innovation: Brown, 2010, pp. 18, 127, 137.

Physical movement: Brown, 2010, p. 151.

Pet: Brown, 2010, p. 152.

Play with Babies

"Well, hello! . . ." Stern, 2002, p. 19.

Stern observes that such play occurs in many cultures. Stern, 2002, pp. 29–31.

Vicariously Enjoy Toddlers' Independent Mastery

Caregiver's unobtrusive presence. Crain, 2003.

Give the Child the Power Position

Rough-and-tumble play. Kennedy-Moore, 2015.

Role reversal in nonhuman animals: Bekoff & Pierce, 2009, pp. 123–24.

Participate in Make-Believe Play

Make-believe play originating from children, not adults. Crain, 2003, pp. 40–41.

Video Games

Brown on video games. Brown, 2010, pp. 183–88.

Chapter 10. Stone Meditations

Epigraph. Lame Deer, 1972, p. 174.

Age of stones. Bjornerud, 2005, pp. 5, 61–62.

Erosion of rocks provided minerals in the oceans, setting the stage for life: Carson, 1991, p. 7. University of Wisconsin-Madison, 2016.

Grahn, 2004.

Appendix A. The Child as Guide

Epigraph: "Genius is..." Baudelaire quoted in Montagu, 1989, p. 177.

Lao Tzu, 1998, p. 64.

Jesus on becoming like children: Matthew, 15:3–4.

A Poet's Vision

Wordsworth grew up in England's Lake District: Wordsworth, 1950.

Sometimes frightened in nature: Wordsworth, 1979, pp. 2, 44.

A "gracious spirit." Wordsworth, 1979, p. 179.

Wordsworth feeling a spirit force in all nature and in himself: Wordsworth, 1979, pp. 79, 87, 88, 489.

Such feelings were strongest in his childhood: Wordsworth, 1979, pp. 433, 489.

Death of Wordsworth's parents and break up of romantic relationship: Parrish, 2019. Disillusionment with the French Revolution, Penguin Poetry Library, 1950, introductory note.

Wordsworth continued to feel nature's soothing presence. Wordsworth, 1979, p. 490.

Quotes from "Ode to Immortality": Wordsworth, 1950.

Alcott

Wordsworth's influence on Alcott: Schreiner, 2006, p. 39.

On Alcott's life and work: Harding, 1982, p. 67; Schreiner, 2006, pp. 35–40, 103–18; Miller, 1990, pp. 89–93.

Alcott's conversations with Thoreau: Thoreau, 1961, p. 111; Harding, 1982, pp. 66–68.

Alcott felt he picked up personal qualities from children: Alcott, 1938, p. 55.

"... on a larger scale..." Peabody, 2005, pp. 19–20.

Thoreau's references to Wordsworth's poetry: Thoreau, 1961, pp. 47, 20, 212.

Artists

On Ruskin: Richardson, 1986, p. 359.

On Impressionism: The Art Story, 2019.

Kandinsky quote: Goldwater, 1986, p. 128.

Klee imitated childhood drawings: Goldwater, 1986, pp. 200–4.

Dewey

Dewey, 1966, p. 50.

Innovative Psychologists

Maslow, 1962, pp. 129–30. See also Crain, 2011, pp. 377–78.

Schachtel, 1959, p. 288. See also Crain, 2011, chapter 15.

Werner: Crain, 2011, p. 98.

Cobb

Cobb's background: Mead, 1977.

Hart, 1979. Moore: Moore & Wong, 1997, p. 81. Sobel, 1993, p. 77.

Newton quote: Cobb, 1977, p. 88.

". . . in some highly evocative way." Cobb, 1959, p. 538.

Berenson quote: Cobb, 1977, p. 32.

Gifted adults return in memory to vivid childhood experiences: Cobb, 1959, p. 539; 1977, p. 87.

Ordinary adults also can benefit: Cobb, 1959, p. 538.

Chawla, 1990.

Some "memories originated in early childhood and adolescence." Chawla, 1990, p. 20.

Wordsworth felt nature provided him with a "holy calm." Wordsworth, 1979, pp. 24, 85.

The Concept of Neoteny

Neoteny refers to the prolongation of childhood: Montagu, 1989, pp. 1, 2, 8, 251.

Cobb's discussion of neoteny: Cobb, 1977, pp. 35–36.

Montagu's lists of neoteny's benefits: Montagu, 1989, pp. 2, 95.

Montagu says most adults have lost childhood qualities: Montagu, 1989, p. 3.

Neoteny needed to meet challenges of the future: Montagu, 1989, pp. 3–5, 61.

A New Breed of Adult

"Whether buying new cars..." Noxon, 2006, p. 2.

Noxon says rejuveniles marry later, postpone childbirth, and live with parents: Noxon, 2006, p. 3.

Culture of children "brims with qualities..." Noxon, 2006, p. 11.

Marriage postponed longer than ever: In 2018, age of first marriage was a record thirty for men and twenty-eight for women. Geiger & Livingston, 2019.

Childbirth in U.S. postponed longer than ever: Ducharme, 2018, compares 2007 and 2017.

Young adults, twenty-five to twenty-nine years of age, living with parent or grandparent was at highest rate in seventy-five years, as of 2016: Kopf, 2018.

Average age of video game player was thirty-three in 2005 and 2018: Entertainment Software Assessment, 2006, 2019.

Most visitors to Disney World were adults without kids. The data on this is imprecise but suggests that adults do still comprise the majority of visitors: Cheatham, 2018; Roen, 2019.

Appendix B. Some Remarkable Strengths of Childhood

Sense of Wonder: Maslow, 1966, p. 100; Schachtel, 1959; Carson, 1998a.

Cobb suggested wonder begins...when babies discover their hands: Cobb, 1977, p. 28.

Piaget's observations: Piaget, 1974, pp. 64–69, 73, 96–97.

Wonder gives way to more realistic outlook at age 7 or so: Crain, 2011, p. 148.

Mahler and coauthors: Mahler, Pine, & Bergman, 1975.

At twelve or thirteen months children begin pretend acts: Singer & Singer, 1990, p. 66.

Playing pirates involves "integrated actions . . ." Singer & Singer, 1990, p. 66.

"The high season of imaginative play." Singer & Singer, 1990, p. 64.

Carson, Montessori, and E. O. Wilson on children's innate love of nature: Crain & Crain, 2014.

Oneness with nature: Shelley, 1951. Crain & Crain, 2014; Cobb, 1959; Cobb, 1977, pp. 32–33; Hart, 1979.

A special affinity to nature seems to last until onset of adolescence. Crain, 2003, pp. 47–52.

A golden period of artistic development," Gardner, 1980, p. 99. See also Crain, 2003, pp. 77–80.

Chukovsky, 1963.

Montessori on child's linguistic abilities: Crain, 2011, pp. 74–75, 351.

Chomsky and the grasp of syntax: Crain, 2011, Ch. 17.

References

Alcott, Amos Bronson, 1938. In Odell Shepard, ed., *The Journals of Bronson Alcott*. Boston: Little, Brown and Company. (Originally written 1826–1882.)

Alexander, Christine, and Margaret Smith, 2018. *The Oxford Companion to the Brontës*. Oxford, U.K.: Oxford University Press.

Ames, Louis Bates, and Joan Ames Chase, 1980. *Don't Push Your Preschooler* (rev. edition). New York: Harper & Row.

Ariès, Philippe, 1962. *Centuries of Childhood*. Translated by Robert Baldick. New York: Knopf.

The Art Story, 2019. "Impressionism." https://www.theartstory .org/movement-impressionism.htm. Downloaded June 30, 2019.

Attenborough, David, 1979. *Life on Earth: A Natural History*. Boston: Little, Brown Co.

Ayers, William, 1993. *To Teach: The Journey of a Teacher*. New York: Teachers College Press.

Bakerman, Jessica, 2018, Jan. 10. "The Rise and Fade of Education's 'Opt Out' Movement." Medium.com. http:// medium.com/s/new-school/the-rise-and-fade-of education-opt -out-movement-13250787e764.

Bateson, Patrick, 2015, January. "Playfulness and Creativity." *Current Biology*, 25 (1). Also available online https://www .sciencedirect.com/science/article/pii/S0960982214011245.

Bekoff, Marc, and Jessica Pierce, 2009. *Wild Justice: The Moral Lives of Animals*. Chicago: University of Chicago Press.

Bjornerud, Marcia, 2005. *Reading the Rocks: The Autobiography of the Earth*. New York: Basic Books.

Bodanis, David, 2000. $E = mc^2$: *A Biography of the World's Most Famous Equation*. New York: Walker & Company.

Brink, Judd, 2020, Sept. 29. "Migrating Mysteries." https://explorebrainerdlakes.com/uncategorized/migration-mysteries/.

Brontë, Charlotte, 1988. "We wove a web in childhood" from poem, "Retrospection." In *The Brontë Sisters: Selected Poems of Charlotte, Emily and Anne Brontë*, edited by Stevie Davies. Manchester, U.K.: Carcenet. (Poem originally written in 1835.)

Brontë, Charlotte, 2011. *Jane Eyre*. New York: Puffin Books. (Originally published in 1847.)

Brontë, Emily, 2014. "To Imagination." In *Bronte Sisters' Poetry: Poems by Anne, Charlotte, and Emily Bronte*. Middletown, DE: n.p. (Originally published in 1846.)

Brooks, Paul, 1989. *The House of Life: Rachel Carson at Work*. Boston: Houghton Mifflin.

Brown, Stuart, 2010. *Play: How It Shapes the Brain, Opens the Imagination, and Invigorates the Soul*. New York: Avery.

Browning, Robert, 2015. "Home-thoughts from abroad." In *Dramatic Romances and Lyrics* by Robert Browning. London: Forgotten Books. (Originally published in 1845.)

Calaprice, Alice, 2011. *The Ultimate Quotable Einstein*. Princeton, NJ: Princeton University Press.

Calaprice, Alice, Daniel Kennefick, and Robert Schulman, 2015. *An Einstein Encyclopedia*. Princeton, NJ: Princeton University Press.

Campbell, Neil, and Jane Reece, 2005. *Biology* (7th ed.). San Francisco: Pearson/Benjamin Cummings.

Carlson, Elof Axel, 1966. *The Gene: A Critical History*. Philadelphia, PA:: W.B. Saunders.

Carson, Rachel L. 1941. *Under the Sea Wind*. New York: Signet.

Carson, Rachel L., 1991. *The Sea Around Us*. New York: Oxford University Press. (Originally published in 1950.)

Carson, Rachel, 1998a. *The Sense of Wonder*. New York: Harper Collins. (Originally published in 1956.)

Carson, Rachel, 1998b. *Lost Woods: The Discovered Writing of Rachel Carson*, edited by Linda Lear. Boston: Beacon Press.

Carson, Rachel, 1998c. *The Edge of the Sea*. Boston: Houghton Mifflin. (Originally published in 1955.)

Carson, Rachel, 2002. *Silent Spring*. Boston: Mariner Books. (Originally published in 1962.)

Chawla, Louise, 1986. "The Ecology of Environmental Memory." *Children's Environments Quarterly 3* (4), 34–41.

Chawla, Louise, 1990. "Ecstatic Places." *Children's Environments Quarterly 7* (4), 18–23.

Cheatham, Antionia, 2018, Sept. 6. "Measuring Travel Behavior at Walt Disney World." Streetlightdata. https://www.streetlightdata.com/measuring-travel-behavior-disney-world/.

Chukovsky Kornei, 1963. *From Two to Five*. Translated and edited by Miriam Morton. Berkeley, CA: University of California Press. (Originally published in 1925.)

Cobb, Edith, 1959. "Work in Progress. The Ecology of Imagination in Childhood." *Daedalus*, 88, 537–49.

Cobb, Edith, 1977. *The Ecology of Imagination in Childhood*. New York: Columbia University Press.

Cornell, Joseph, 1998. *Sharing Nature with Children*. Nevada City, CA: Dawn Publications.

Crain, William, 2003. *Reclaiming Childhood: Letting Children Be Children in our Achievement-Oriented Society*. New York: Henry Holt.

Crain, William, 2011. *Theories of Development: Concepts and Applications* (6th ed.). Boston: Prentice-Hall.

Crain, William, 2014. *The Emotional Lives of Animals and Children: Insights from a Farm Sanctuary*. San Francisco: Turning Stone Press.

Crain, William and Ellen, 2014. "The Benefits of the Green Environment." In *Textbook of Children's Environmental Health*, edited by Philip Landrigan and Ruth Etzel. Oxford U.K.: Oxford University Press.

Darwin, Charles, 1958. *The Autobiography of Charles Darwin, 1809–1882*. New York: Norton. (Originally published in 1887.)

Davies, Stevie, 2014. Introduction. In *The Brontë Sisters: Selected Poems*, edited by Stevie Davies. Manchester, U.K.: Carcenet.

Dewey, John, 1966. *Democracy and Education*. New York: Free Press. (Originally published in 1916.)

Ducharme, Jaime, 2018, Oct. 17. "Americans Are Having Fewer Kids—and Having Them Later in Life, Report Says." *Time*. http://time.com/5425376/fertility-rates-report/.

Dukas, Helen, and Banesh Hoffmann, 1979. *Albert Einstein: The Human Side*. Princeton, NJ: Princeton University Press.

Einstein, Albert, 1934. *Letters to Solovine: 1906–1955*. New York: Philosophical Library.

Einstein, Albert, 1959. "Autobiographical Notes." Translated by P.A. Schilpp. In *Albert Einstein: Philosopher-Scientist*, Vol. 1, edited by Paul Arthur Schilpp. New York: Harper Torchbooks.

Einstein, Albert, 1982. *Ideas and Opinions*. Edited by Carl Seelig and translated by Sonja Bargmann. New York: Three Rivers Press.

Einstein, Albert, 2015. "What I Believe." In *An Einstein Encyclopedia*, edited by Alice Calaprice, Daniel Kennefick, and Robert Schulman. Princeton, NJ: Princeton University Press. (Originally published in 1930.)

Eisen, George, 1990. *Children and Play in the Holocaust: Games among the Shadow*. Amherst: University of Massachusetts Press.

Ellenberger, Henri F., 1958. "A Clinical Introduction to Psychiatric Phenomenology and Existential Analysis." In *Existence: A New Dimension in Psychiatry and Psychology*, edited by Rollo May, Ernest Angel, and Henri F. Ellenberger. New York: Basic Books.

Emerson, Ralph Waldo, 2003a. *Nature*. In *Nature and Other Writings*, edited by Peter Turner. Boston: Shambhala. (Originally published in 1836.)

Emerson, Ralph Waldo, 2003b. "Self Reliance." In *Nature and Other Writings*, edited by Peter Turner. Boston: Shambhala. (Originally published in 1841.)

Emerson, Ralph Waldo, 2003c. "The Over-Soul." In *Nature and Other Writings*, edited by Peter Turner. Boston: Shambhala. (Originally published in 1841.)

Entertainment Software Association, 2006. "2006 Essential Facts about the Computer and Video Game Industry." https://library.princeton.edu/sites/default/files/2006.pdf.

Entertainment Software Association, 2019. "2019 Essential Facts about the Computer and Video Game Industry." https://www.theesa.com/resource/essential-facts-about-the-computer-and-video-game-industry-2019/.

Erikson, Erik H., 1982. "Psychoanalytic Reflections on Einstein's Centenary." In *Albert Einstein: Historical and Cultural Perspectives*, edited by Gerald Holton and Yehuda Elkana. Princeton, NJ: Princeton University Press.

Erikson, Joan M., 1988. *Wisdom and the Senses: The Way of Creativity*. New York: W. W. Norton & Company.

Feuer, Lewis S., 1974. *Einstein and the Generations of Science.* New York: Basic Books.

Fowler, R. Clarke, 2018. "The Disappearance of Child-directed Activities and Teachers' Autonomy from Massachusetts' Kindergartens." Defending the Early Years. https://dey.org/wp-content/uploads/2019/03/ma_kindergartens_final.pdf

Gardner, Howard, 1980. *Artful Scribbles: The Significance of Children's Drawings.* New York: Basic Books.

Gardner, Howard, 1982. *Developmental Psychology: An Introduction* (2nd ed.). Boston: Little, Brown & Co., p. 253.

Gardner, Howard, 1994. *The Arts and Human Development: A Psychological Study of the Artistic Process.* New York: Basic Books.

Gaskell, Elizabeth. 1997. *The Life of Charlotte Brontë.* London, U.K.: Penguin Books. (Originally published in 1857).

Geggel, Laura, 2014, Sept. 17. "Chimps Are Naturally Violent, Study Suggests." *Live Science.* https://www.livescience.com/47885-chimpanzee-aggression-evolution.html.

Geiger, Abigail W., and Gretchen Livingston, 2019, Feb. 13. "8 Facts about Love and Marriage in America." Pew Research Center, http://www.pewresearch.org/fact-tank/2019/02/13/8-facts-about-love-and-marriage/.

Gibran, Kahlil, 2019. *The Prophet.* Project Gutenberg EBook #58585, p. 42. http://www.gutenberg.org/files/58585/58585-h/58585-h.htm#link41 (Originally published in 1923.)

Glenister, Pete, and Scott Wilk, 1986. "Invisible to You." U.K.: Werner/Chappell Music, Inc.

Goldberg, E., 1999. *Reason for Hope* (video). Twin Cities Public Television.

Goldwater, Robert, 1986. *Primitivism in Modern Art* (enlarged edition). Cambridge, MA: The Belknap Press of Harvard University Press. (Originally published in 1938.)

Goodall, Jane, 1986. *The Chimpanzees of Gombe*. Cambridge, MA: Harvard University Press.

Goodall, Jane, 1996. *My Life with the Chimpanzees*. New York: A Byron Preiss Book. (Originally published in 1988.)

Goodall, Jane, 2000. *In the Shadow of Man*. Boston: A Mariner Book.

Goodall, Jane, with Phillip Berman, 2003. *Reason for Hope*. New York: Grand Central Publishing.

gotQuestions?org, https://www.gotquestions.org/Jesus-and-children.html.

Grahn, Patrick 2004, May. Children's pre-school environments. Design for Active Childhoods, The Natural Learning Initiative, College of Design, North Carolina State University.

Gutek, Gerald Lee, 1999. *Pestalozzi and Education*. Prospect Heights, IL: Waveland Press.

Harding, Walter, 1982. *The Days of Henry Thoreau: A Biography*. New York: Dover.

Harman, Claire, 2015. *Charlotte Brontë: A Life*. Falkirk, U.K.: Viking.

Hart, Roger, 1979. *Children's Experience of Place*. New York: Irvington.

Higgins, Richard, 2017. *Thoreau and the Language of Trees*. Oakland: University of California Press.

Hoffman, Edward, 1992. *Visions of Innocence: Spiritual and Inspirational Experiences of Childhood*. Boston: Shambala.

Hoffmann, Banesh, 1972. *Albert Einstein: Creator & Rebel*. New York: New American Library.

The Holy Bible. The New Testament. English Standard Edition.

Isaacson, Walter, *Einstein: His Life and Universe*. New York: Simon & Schuster Paperbacks.

James, William, 2020. *The Varieties of Religious Experience: A Study in Human Nature.* New York: Library of America Paperback Classics. (Originally published in 1902).

Jane Goodall Institute U.K. 2020, Feb. 14. Biography. https://www.janegoodall.org.uk/jane-goodall/biography.

Jerome, Fred, and Rodger Taylor, 2006. *Einstein on Race and Racism.* New Brunswick, NJ: Rutgers University Press.

Johnson, Cathy, 1991. *The Naturalist's Path: Beginning the Study of Nature.* New York: Walker and Company.

Johnson, Merkes E. 2020. "Silurian Period." Encyclopedia Britannica. https://www.britannica/Science/Silurian-Period.

Kaku, Michio, 2004. *Einstein's Cosmos: How Albert Einstein's Vision Transformed Our Understanding of Space and Time.* New York: Atlas Books.

Kane, Jeffrey, 1995. "Educational Reform and the Dangers of Triumphant Rhetoric." In *Educational Freedom for a Democratic Society: A Critique of National Standards, Goals, and Curriculum,* edited by Ron Miller. Brandon, VT: Resource Center for Redesigning Education.

Kaplan, David, 2021, Jan. 5. "How Did Life Begin on Earth?" *Quanta Magazine* video. https://www.quantamagazine.org/how-did-life-begin-on-earth/.

Kennedy-Moore, Eileen, 2015, June 30. "Do Boys Need Rough and Tumble Play?" *Psychology Today,* https://www.psychologytoday.com/blog/growing-friendships/201506/do-boys-need-rough-and-tumble-play.

Kirylo, James D., 2015, Feb. 5. "Why My Son Will Opt Out of PARCC." Talk about the South. http://talkaboutthesouth.com/uncaptioned/201/.

Kopf, Dan, 2018, Apr. 10. "The Share of American Adults Living with Their Parents Is the Highest in 75 Years." https://qz.com/1248081/the-share-of-americans-25-29-living-with-parents-is-the-highest-in-75-years/.

Lame Deer, John, and Richard Erdoes, 1972. *Lame Deer: Seeker of Visions*. New York: Washington Square Press.

Lao Tzu, 1998. *Tao Te Ching: A Book about the Way and the Power of the Way*. Edited by Ursula K. Le Guin. Boston: Shambhala.

Lear, Linda, 1997, *Rachel Carson: Witness for Nature*. Boston: Mariner Books.

Lear, Linda, 1998. Introduction and notes. In *Lost Woods: The Discovered Writing of Rachel Carson*, edited by Linda Lear. Boston: Beacon Press.

Levin, Diane E., and Judith L. Van Hoorn, 2016. *Teachers Speak Out: How School Reforms Are Failing Low-Income Children*. Defending the Early Years. http://www.deyproject.org/uploads/1/5/5/7/15571834/tacherspeakfinal_rgb.pdf

Loewer, Peter, 2009. *Thoreau's Garden: Native Plants for the American Landscape*. Rock Hill, SC: Bella Rosa Books.

Mahler, Margaret S., Fred Pine, and Anni Bergman, 1975. *The Psychological Birth of the Human Infant*. London: Hutchinson.

Marshall, Michael, 2016, Oct. 31. "The Secret of How Life on Earth Began." BBC. http://www.bbc.com/earth/story/20161026-the-secret-of-how-life-on-earth-began.

Maslow, Abraham H., 1954. *Motivation and Personality*. New York: Harper & Brothers.

Maslow, Abraham H., 1962. *Toward a Psychology of Being*. Princeton, NJ: Insight Book.

Maslow, Abraham, 1966. *The Psychology of Science: A Reconnaissance*. Chicago: Gateway.

Maslow, Abraham, 1971. *The Farther Reaches of Human Nature*. New York: Esalen Books.

Mead, Margaret, 1977. Introduction. In *The Ecology of Imagination in Childhood* by Edith Cobb. New York: Columbia University Press.

Miller, Ron, 1990. *What Are Schools For?* Brandon, VT: Holistic Education Press.

Montagu, Ashley, 1989. *Growing Young* (2nd ed.). New York: Bergin & Garvey Publishers.

Moore, Kathleen Dean, 2008. "The Truth of the Barnacles: Rachel Carson and the Moral Significance of Wonder." In *Rachel Carson: Legacy and Challenge*, edited by Lisa H. Sideris and Kathleen Dean Moore. Albany: State University of New York Press.

Moore, Robin C., and Herbert Wong, 1997. *Natural Learning: The Life History of an Environmental Schoolyard: Creating Environments for Rediscovering Nature's Way of Teaching*. Berkeley, CA: MIG Communications.

Noxon, Christopher, 2006. *Rejuvenile: Kickball, Cartoons, Cupcakes, and the Reinvention of the American Grown-Up*. New York: Crown Publishers.

Ocean Explorer, 2017, July 21. National Oceanic and Atmospheric Administration.

Organ, Christine, 2016, Mar. 7. "Why I'm Considering Opting My Son Out of Standardized Tests." Scarymommy.com. https://www.scraymommy.com/standardized-testing-opt-out/

Overgaard, Søren, 2004. "Husserl and Heidegger on Being in the World." Copenhagen, Denmark: Danish National Research Foundation: Center for Subjectivity Research.

Parrish, Stephen Maxfield, 2019, May 17. William Wordsworth. *Encyclopedia Britannica*. https//www.britannica.com/biography/William-Wordsworth.

Peabody, E. 2005. *Record of a School: Exemplifying the General Principles of Spiritual Culture*. Bedford, MA: Applewood Books. (Originally published in 1845).

Penguin Poetry Library (1950). Introductory Comment. In *Wordsworth*, edited by W. E. Williams. London: Penguin.

Pestalozzi, Johann Heinrich, 1951. *The Education of Man: Aphorisms*. Translated by Heinz and Ruth Norden. New York: Philosophical Library.

Peterson, Dale, 2006. *Jane Goodall: The Woman Who Redefined Man*. Boston: Houghton Mifflin.

Piaget, Jean, 1974. *The Origins of Intelligence in Children*. Translated by Margaret Cook. New York: International Universities Press. (Originally published in 1936).

Power, Margaret, 1991. *The Egalitarians—Human and Chimpanzee*. Cambridge, U.K.: Cambridge University Press.

Ratchford, Fannie Elizabeth, 1949. *The Brontes' Web of Childhood*. New York: Columbia University Press.

Read, Herbert, 1940. *Annals of Innocence and Experience*. London: Faber & Faber.

Richardson, Robert D., Jr., 1986. *Henry Thoreau: A Life of the Mind*. Berkeley: University of California Press.

Robinson, David M., 2004. *Natural Life: Thoreau's Worldly Transcendentalism*. Ithaca, NY: Cornell University Press.

Robinson, Edward, 1983. *The Original Vision: A Study of the Religious Experience of Children*. New York: Seabury Press.

Roen, Terry, 2019, Mar. 24. "Theme Park Demographics Changing." *Orlando Rising*, https://orlando-rising.com /theme-park-demographics-changing-higher-incomes-and-more -millennials/.

Schachtel, Ernest, 1959. *Metamorphosis: On the Development of Affect, Perception, Attention, and Memory*. New York: Basic Books.

Schreiner, Samuel A., Jr., 2006. *The Concord Quartet: Alcott, Emerson, Hawthorne, Thoreau, and the Friendship That Freed the American Mind*. Hoboken, NJ: Wiley.

Shanker, Gwendolyn, 2016, Aug. 25. "A Slithery Ocean Mystery." *Oceanus*. https://www.whoi.edu/oceanus/feature/a -slithery-ocean-mystery/.

Shelley, Percy Bysshe, 1951. "On life." In *Shelley: Selected Poetry and Prose*, edited by Carlos Baker. New York: Modern Library. (Work originally published in 1840.)

Shepard, Odell, 1961. Comment. In *The Heart of Thoreau's Journals*, edited by Odell Shepard. New York: Dover.

Singer, Dorothy and Jerome, 1990. *The House of Make-Believe: Children's Play and the Developing Imagination*. Cambridge, MA: Harvard University Press.

Smith, Gina, 2005. *The Genomics Age: How DNA Technology Is Transforming the Way We Live and Who We Are*. New York: AMACOM.

Smith, Luther E., Jr., 2007. *Howard Thurman: The Mystic as Prophet* (3rd ed.). Richmond, IN: Friends United Meeting.

Snyder, Gary, 1992. "For all." In *No Nature: New and Selected Poems*. New York: Pantheon

Sobel, David, 1993. *Children's Special Places: Exploring the Role of Forts, Dens, and Bush Houses in Middle Childhood*. Tucson, AZ: Zephyr Press.

Sobel, David, 2008. "Appareled in Celestial Light: Transcendent Nature Experiences in Childhood." *Encounter: Education for Meaning and Social Justice* 21, 14–19.

Solovine, Maurice, 1934. Introduction by Maurice Solovine. In *Letters to Solovine: 1906–1955* by Albert Einstein. New York: Philosophical Library.

Stanford, Craig Britton, 2018. *The New Chimpanzee: A Twenty-First Century Portrait of Our Closest Ancestor*. Cambridge, MA: Harvard University Press.

Stern, Daniel N., 2002. *The First Relationship: Infant and Mother*. Cambridge, MA: Harvard University Press.

Sussman, Robert, and Joshua Marhack, 2010. "Are Humans Inherently Killers?" Center for Global Nonkilling. http://nonkilling.org/pdf/wp1.pdf.

Thoreau, Henry David, 1961. *The Heart of Thoreau's Journals.* Edited by Odell Shepard. New York: Dover.

Thoreau, Henry David, 1962. *The Journal of Henry D. Thoreau in Fourteen Volumes Bound as Two. Volumes VIII–XIV (November 1855–1861).* Edited by Bradford Torrey. New York: Dover.

Thoreau, Henry David, 1978. *The Natural Man.* Edited by Robert Epstein and Sherry Phillips. Wheaton, IL: Quest Books.

Thoreau, Henry David, 1981a. *Walden.* In *Walden and Other Writings by Henry David Thoreau,* edited by Joseph Wood Krutch. Toronto, Canada: Bantam. (Originally published in 1854.)

Thoreau, Henry David, 1981b. "Life without Principle." In *Walden and Other Writings by Henry David Thoreau,* edited by Joseph Wood Krutch. Toronto, Canada: Bantam. (Originally published in 1863.)

Thoreau, Henry David, 1981c. "Civil Disobedience." In *Walden and Other Writings by Henry David Thoreau,* edited by Joseph Wood Krutch. Toronto, Canada: Bantam. (Originally published in 1849.)

Thoreau, Henry David, 1984. *Journal, Vol. 2: 1842–1848.* Edited by Robert Sattelmeyer. Princeton, NJ: Princeton University Press.

Thoreau, Henry David, 1999a. *Uncommon Learning: Thoreau on Education.* Edited by Martin Bickman. Boston: A Mariner Original.

Thoreau, Henry David, 1999b. *Material Faith: Henry David Thoreau on Science.* Edited by Laura Dassaw Walls. Boston: A Mariner Original.

Thoreau, Henry David, 2010. *Walking.* Lexington, KY: Cricket Hill Books. (Originally published in 1862.)

Thoreau, Henry David, 2016a. *The Journal of Henry David Thoreau, Vol. 4*, May 1852–February 1853. Edited by Bradford Torrey and Francis Henry Allen. Sportsman's Vintage Press.

Thoreau, Henry David, 2016b. *A Week on the Concord and Merrimack Rivers*. Middletown, DE: McAllister Editions. (Work originally published in 1849.)

Thoreau, Henry David, 2019, Jan. 27. "Night and Moonlight." In *Excursions*. Middletown, DE: Project Gutenberg EBook of Excursions.

Thurman, Howard, 1979. *With Head and Heart: The Autobiography of Howard Thurman*. San Diego, CA: Harvest.

Thurman, Howard, 1981. *Meditations of the Heart*. Boston: Beacon Press. (Originally published in 1953.)

Thurman, Howard, 1996. *Jesus and the Disinherited*. Boston: Beacon Press. (Originally published in 1949.)

Thurman, Howard, 1998. In *A Strange Freedom: The Best of Howard Thurman on Religious Experience and Public Life*, edited by Walter E. Fluker and Catherine Tumber. Boston: Beacon Press.

Tumber, Catherine, and Walter E. Fluker, eds., 1998. Introduction. In *A Strange Freedom: The Best of Howard Thurman on Religious Experience and Public Life*. Boston: Beacon Press.

University of Wisconsin-Madison. 2016, Sept. 26. "Life in Ancient Oceans Enabled by Erosion from Land." *Science Daily*. www.sciencedaily.com/releases/2016/09/160926221617.htm.

U.S. National Library of Medicine. (n.d.). Profiles in Science. The Marshall W. Nirenberg Papers. Biographical Information. https://profiles.nlm.nih.gov/JJ/. Retrieved June 18, 2018.

Vallentin, Antonina, 1954. *The Drama of Albert Einstein*. Translated by Moura Budberg. Garden City, NY: Doubleday& Co, Inc.

Walls, Laura Dassow, 2017. *Henry David Thoreau: A Life*. Chicago: University of Chicago Press.

Watts, Alan, 1951. *The Wisdom of Insecurity*. New York: Vantage.

White, Michael, and John Gribbin, 1994. *Einstein: A Life in Science*. New York: Dutton.

Williams, Juan, and Quinton Hosford Dixie, 2003. *This Far by Faith: Stories from the African-American Religious Experience*. New York: Amistad.

Wilson, Colleen. 2019, Apr. 1. "What to Know as 2019 State Tests Begin." *Poughkeepsie Journal*, front page.

Wilson, Edward O., 1993. "Biophilia and the Conservation Ethic." In *The Biophilia Hypothesis*, edited by Stephen R. Kellert and Edward O. Wilson. Washington, DC: Island Press.

Witherell, Elizabeth, with Elizabeth Dubrulle, 1995. "The Life and Times of Henry David Thoreau." In *The Writings of Henry D. Thoreau*. http://thoreaulibrary.ucsb.edu/thoreau_life.html (retrieved July 1, 2016).

Wordsworth, William, 1950. *Wordsworth: Poems*. Edited by W. E. Williams. London, U.K.: Penguin Books.

Wordsworth, William, 1979. *The Prelude 1799, 1805, 1850*. Edited by Jonathan Wordsworth, M. H. Abrams, and Stephen Gill. New York: W.W. Norton & Company.

Wu, Katherine J., 2020, Jan. 8. "Immersing Yourself in Jane Goodall's Wondrous, Chimpanzee-Filled Life." *Smithsonian Magazine*. https://www.smithsonianmag.com/smart-news/immerse-yourself-jane-goodalls-wondrous-chimpanzee-filled-life-new-exhibit-180973919/.

Zwinger, Ann H., 1991. Introduction. In *The Sea Around Us* by Rachel Carson. New York: Oxford University Press.

Acknowledgments

Perhaps the strongest encouragement writers and scholars can receive is others' interest in their work. I would like to mention just a few of those whose interest has recently meant a great deal to me: Elizabeth Goodenough, Richard Lewis, Nancy Carlsson-Page, Marc Bekoff, Carol Garboden Murray, Tovah Klein, and my colleagues at CCNY and its Workshop Center and the Sarah Lawrence College Child Development Institute. I am also grateful to my family for their inspiration and humor. This is my second book with Turning Stone Press, and I thank the staff for their skillful efforts.

Name Index

Author Biography

William Crain is a professor emeritus of psychology at The City College of New York. His writings include the book *Reclaiming Childhood: Letting Children Be Children in Our Achievement-Oriented Society*. With his wife Ellen, Bill founded Safe Haven Farm Sanctuary, which gives a lifelong home to farm animals rescued from slaughter. Bill and Ellen have three grown children and six grandchildren.